SURVIVE
IN
BUSINESS

HOW TO
TURN YOUR
STRUGGLING BUSINESS
AROUND

Steve Lloyd

Survive in Business Pty Ltd ACN 109 655 138
P.O. Box 496, Ballina. NSW. Australia 2478

www.surviveinbusiness.com

Published November 2020.

ISBN
Paperback: 978-0-6489719-0-0
Epub: 978-0-6489719-1-7
Mobi: 978-0-6489719-2-4

Cover images © Rangizzz, George D. via Bigstock.com

Managing editor: Belinda Pollard
Copyeditor: Alix Kwan

DISCLAIMER

Preface

Managing a business that is in decline or struggling is very different to managing a healthy business. It can be a very stressful experience and it is often difficult to know what to do or where to go for help. This book has been written specifically for the owners and managers of businesses that are going through tough times and experiencing financial troubles. It has been designed to provide practical, easy-to-follow guidance to help you identify and understand what is causing the problems with your business; to help you decide what steps you may be able to take to make it right; and to help you develop and implement a turnaround plan.

The content of this book is the distillation of more than 30 years' experience in working with, and in, businesses experiencing difficulties. In that time, I have seen many businesses fail. I have learned that there is a significant degree of commonality between the causes of most business failures. Many of the business failures I have seen could have been avoided if decisive action had been taken earlier. Indeed, one of the most critical factors in a successful turnaround is early recognition, and acknowledgement that there is a problem that needs to be fixed.

Of course, the individual circumstances of every business and every business manager will be different, so it is important to adapt the ideas, strategies and processes outlined in this book to the individual circumstances and context of your business and yourself. Be prepared to supplement the guidance in this book with expert advice and support as required. By following a disciplined, decisive and timely approach to understanding and responding to the problems being faced by your business, you will maximise the prospects of a successful turnaround.

Steve Lloyd

Success is not final;
failure is not fatal:
it is the courage to continue
that counts.

Winston Churchill

Contents

Introduction

Businesses that are failing today are failing for the same reasons that caused businesses to fail in the past. We can learn from the experiences of those who have failed before. Equally, there is much to learn from those who have successfully restored their businesses to good health. Some of the most successful businessmen in history have failed in business before they ultimately succeeded. Walt Disney's first animation company went broke. Henry Ford's first two car companies failed. Bill Gates' first business venture failed and a number of Richard Branson's Virgin spin-offs have also failed. For these people, and many others, business failure has been a character-building experience from which they have learned – and from which they have rebounded.

But let's be honest here. For the vast majority of business owners and managers whose businesses have failed, the experience has been a debilitating one. The most difficult position a businessperson can find themselves in is when their business is on the brink of collapse. It is a time when managers are faced with having to make some of the most difficult and unpalatable decisions of their lives. Yet, it is a management experience for which no training is provided. Very few managers have any experience in managing these situations.

A business in trouble can damage staff morale, disrupt business operations and destroy business relationships. It can be a period of great stress, often one where managers are confronted with uncertainty, conflict, harassment, and legal threats, while also having to deal with the myriad of complex issues that can emerge, both professional and personal. You may find yourself not only fighting to save your business, but also fighting to save your staff, your home, your family and your reputation. The very serious consequences of business failure make it an experience to be avoided.

By far the most important step in managing a business that is in trouble is to recognise and acknowledge the problem as early as possible, and be honest with yourself about the fact that there is a crisis to be managed. The biggest mistakes you can make when your business experiences problems are to deny that a problem exists or to assume that the situation will correct itself. You should not wait until your bank knocks on the door to take decisive action. Nor should you expect that your suppliers, customers and financiers will continue to support you if you don't take action. You must be proactive in securing their support.

A business in trouble usually presents a range of issues that often require urgent attention. By the time a business gets to the point where it is clearly in serious trouble there are rarely any easy solutions. There are times when the problems confronting a business can seem insurmountable. Sometimes they are insurmountable – but not often. In most cases there are strategies and opportunities available that can provide solutions. There is usually no quick remedy. Turnarounds can take time and always require significant effort and total commitment.

It is important to manage the situation, rather than allowing the situation to manage you. It is easy to fall into the trap of fighting scrub fires while letting the house burn down. You must effectively manage your business if you wish to retain control of the business. That doesn't mean there isn't a place for professional advisers (including, in some circumstances, administrators appointed by you) in developing and working through your turnaround plans. In fact, I would strongly encourage you to take advice from experts both as a source of strategic advice and to give credibility to your turnaround plan. It simply means that you should make the key decisions, using these professionals to your advantage, as part of a considered strategy to successfully turn your business around.

Your approach to resolving the problems you are experiencing must be disciplined and structured. If not, the stresses of your situation will distract you, weaken your resolve, and potentially lead to a disastrous outcome. There will be significant emotional pressures working against you, stresses and emotions that you will probably not be familiar with and that you may not be well equipped to handle alone. These should not be ignored. It is important to share the burden and seek support through this difficult time.

Successfully turning around a business requires the application of both a different mindset and a different skill set to those that apply to running a business under normal circumstances. The manner in which you handle the difficulties that confront you, or will confront you, in these circumstances will define not only the future of your business but, in all likelihood, your own future for many years to come.

The message here is that you must act decisively and take the initiative to understand the problems, develop a plan and drive the resolution strategy relentlessly until you succeed. The fact that you are reading this book means you are astute enough to acknowledge that your business has, or may have, problems that might lead to failure if those problems are not addressed.

1. Why do businesses fail?

The managers of today are not inventing new ways to fail; they are making the same mistakes as their predecessors. Businesses are failing today for the same reasons that businesses failed 100 years ago.

Why do businesses fail? This is not a terribly difficult question to answer – the vast majority of businesses fail because they simply run out of money. They reach a point where they are unable to pay their expenses, or pay staff, or meet their taxes, or repay their debts. If this condition continues, someone will eventually take action to bring the business to an end, either via the appointment of an external administrator to the business, or via a decision by the proprietors of the business to shut down.

Why do businesses run out of money? Generally, because of financial losses or because they don't effectively manage the financial resources available to them. Financial losses, whether they be trading losses or the result of an extraordinary event, consume the assets of a business and impact upon its capacity to fund its activities. Poor management of the short-term assets and liabilities of a business (its "working capital"), can result in a business (even a profitable business) being cash-starved and unable to fund its activities.

Looking back through my experience, most businesses that I have seen fail actually failed because they did not recognise and respond in a timely manner to events that gave rise to these problems. In most cases, financial losses and/or poor management of working capital are not fatal to the business unless there is a corresponding failure to develop and implement responses to overcome these problems. That's why, provided you haven't left it too late, there is hope that your business can be restored to good health.

Typically, business failure is precipitated when an event occurs that triggers a series of consequent events which cascade into failure. There are many different events that might occur to trigger the downward spiral. An economic downturn, actions by competitors, substitute products, critical breakdowns, weather events, changes to laws, changes in consumer tastes, and technological change are just a few. Every business has been or will be, at one time or another, subject to one or more events that, left unchecked, could be potentially fatal to the business.

Let's consider a simple example. A business loses an important contract because a competitor offers the customer a lower price. This causes sales to decline significantly to the point where the business incurs trading losses because it no longer has sufficient revenue to pay its fixed costs. The loss of the contract is the originating event that triggers a downturn in sales. It is likely that the business has alternative income streams and alternative opportunities to secure replacement income; or that it has the option of reducing its costs to match its reduced level of income so as to avoid or minimise trading losses. But securing a new contract, or contracts, will take time, and the business must survive by meeting all of its costs until the new contract is secured. It may also have to invest in new plant, retooling, restocking or unbudgeted marketing to secure new work, all of which have to be funded. A business without capacity to fund itself through this period is more vulnerable to failure. Indeed, lack of working capital may mean that the business does not have the capacity to survive even if it has alternative opportunities to secure new contracts. The response of the business to losing the contract, and its capacity to fund itself, will determine whether the loss of the contract is ultimately fatal.

The decline of a business generally occurs over time. It may take a number of years to reach the end game. During the decline, the position of the business will progressively deteriorate. Threats to the survival of the business tend to accumulate and the momentum towards failure builds like a snowball.

Trading losses

In my 30 years of working with businesses going through difficulties, trading losses have been the most common underlying cause of the failure of businesses.

When the trading revenue of a business (sales) exceeds the costs of earning that revenue (expenses) a business makes a profit. Conversely, trading losses arise when the sales revenue of the business is less than the expenses incurred in earning that revenue.

Losses are not just negative numbers at the bottom of a profit and loss account. They are not just events that are to be regretted and, hopefully, forgotten. Losses destroy value in a business. Trading losses deplete the resources of the business, making it more vulnerable to failure. If losses are substantial enough or continue long enough, the assets of the business will be depleted until there are insufficient assets remaining to fund the operations of the business, and the business will fail.

I have been surprised over the years by how many owners and managers of small and medium enterprises ("SMEs") do not appreciate the impact of losses on their business. Often, they have not appeared to know that their business is making losses. This is usually because trading losses do not necessarily immediately impact on cash flow but, instead, are "hidden" in increases in creditors or tax liabilities, reduced stock levels, increased debt or other changes to non-cash working capital accounts. Financial accounts can provide insight into these changes, but many SMEs do not prepare proper financial accounts on a timely basis. Often, financial accounts are only prepared to meet statutory reporting or tax obligations or the expectations of the bank. Without proper accounts, trading losses can go unnoticed for some time. Some business owners have even suggested to me that losses can be a good outcome because "at least I don't have to pay any income tax". The longer you fail to recognise that your business is making losses before taking action to restore profitability, the greater the impact of the losses will be, and the more difficult it will be for your business to recover.

Making profits is a critical goal in any and every plan to survive in business. A business that does not make profits cannot survive in the long run. Whatever else you need to do to get through the difficulties that your business is currently experiencing, your business must come out of those difficulties making profits.

Common causes of trading losses

Trading losses arise when a business fails to generate sufficient sales revenue to cover the costs of making those sales. The most common causes of trading losses are:

- a decline in sales revenue
- a reduction in profit margins
- excessive overheads.

Sales in decline

The most common cause of trading losses is a sustained decline in sales. Falling sales can be caused by a number of factors which are generally easy to recognise. Competitive forces are most often the reason that sales decline. Businesses operate in a competitive environment with, in most cases, a finite market. Businesses often take steps to increase their share of the market by seeking to take market share from their competitors. The most common techniques used to take a competitor's market share include:

- price discounting
- entering the geographic market of a competitor
- product innovation
- customer service innovation
- aggressive marketing and sales techniques.

Aside from the actions of competitors, there are a number of other possible causes of declining sales, including:

- macro-economic events, such as an economic or industry downturn, resulting in reduced expenditure by customers as a result of rising unemployment, loss of confidence, uncertainty or risk aversion, stock reduction, and the deferral or suspension of capital expenditures
- technological change, allowing competitors to introduce improved products or new alternative/replacement products that compete with your products or are cheaper to produce
- changes in consumer preferences or tastes. These changes are most evident in clothing but also occur in many other aspects of daily life including food (look, for example, at the emergence of gluten-free, vegetarian and vegan eating habits in recent years and the emergence of pre-prepared, home-delivered meal packs)
- changes to the public perception of your business. Price increases, unreliable supply, product quality issues and poor customer service are all examples of actions by businesses that can have a material impact on sales. These perceptions may even extend to employment practices, environmental responsibility or even management integrity. Social media has made reputational risk a much more potent threat to businesses in recent times
- loss of a major contract

- loss of a key customer
- internal disruption – machinery breakdown, supply interruption, loss of key staff, union action and other internal events can result in a disruption to sales
- lack of management focus which, without an adequate response, allows any or all of the above events to gain traction and cause reduced sales for the business.

A permanent or longer-term decline in sales is usually a result of events external to the business. These are events that are not within the immediate control of management. They are events that must be prepared for, and responded to, rather than events that can be prevented.

A fall in sales resulting from internal causes such as machinery breakdown or other events that affect production will generally only have a temporary impact on sales. Management can usually control or limit the impact of these risks and manage the remediation of the causes.

Loss of a major contract, the collapse of a key customer or similar one-off events can also have an impact on sales. The impact can be more severe where the business has a material dependency (concentration) on a small number of contracts or customers.

Many businesses are subject to seasonal influences. Agricultural businesses are the most notable group impacted by seasonal variations but other businesses, from food producers to clothing retailers, can have their sales impacted by seasonal conditions. An unseasonably cold summer may reduce sales of ice creams or sunscreen. Sales of swimsuits, lawn mowers and boats may also be affected. An unseasonably warm winter might reduce the sales of heaters or fuel oil and increase tourism in beach areas. A severe weather event may cause a disruption in production, or transport. Sales fluctuations due to seasonal variations are not usually fatal and are not necessarily symptoms of a deteriorating business, although they may cause impacts that could have longer-term or permanently detrimental impacts on the business. It is possible, for example, that the loss of sales from one very cold summer may put an ice cream store out of business as it has to survive for a year before the next peak season arises.

Declining sales are a significant warning sign, but most businesses that have falling sales will not fail. Many businesses impacted by declining sales either find new markets or achieve profitability at the reduced level of sales by increasing margins or reducing overheads. Declining sales are usually only a threat to the business where management is unable, unwilling, or otherwise fails to respond.

Every business has a break-even sales level based on its prevailing overhead (fixed cost) structure. If the sales level falls below the break-even point, the business will start to make losses. If overhead costs are reduced, the sales required for the business to break even will be lowered. When sales are declining, direct costs will generally reduce automatically, driven by the reduced internal demand for direct inputs; although there may be a time lag while the inventory of production inputs is reduced and some conscious cost reductions may be required. Overheads must also be reduced in a timely manner if losses are to be avoided. Unlike direct costs, overheads will not automatically reduce as sales fall because there is no direct or immediate link between sales and overheads. Overhead reductions require conscious and proactive action by management. It is not always easy for management to make these decisions, as they may be uncertain as to whether the decline in sales is temporary or permanent.

Looking back at our ice cream store, how does management respond to the first cold week in summer? Do they reduce purchases in anticipation of continuing subdued demand, or do they assume the cold snap will end and sales will return to normal? If they destock too quickly they may not be able to meet demand if the weather gets hot. If they don't de-stock and the weather remains cold, they may have to throw out excess stock.

When sales decline in any business, retaining excessive productive capacity, stock, and overheads in anticipation of a future increase in demand may be fatal. On the other hand, reducing the productive capacity of the business may make it unable (or slow) to respond to an increase in demand for its products or services. This means customer demand may go unsatisfied, potentially opening the door for competitors to take your customers. Management are constantly required to make judgements about future demand and to respond accordingly by adjusting productive capacity, stock and overheads. Almost always, responses to a decline in sales will require careful consideration and difficult decisions that will rarely prove to be perfectly correct.

These days the internet facilitates open price competition for almost every product and service on an international stage. The internet also allows consumers to view and understand competing products and services much more readily than was the case in the past. Alternative products that perform the same or similar functions to your products are readily identifiable and accessible. Geographic barriers to competition are also disappearing. It is no longer necessary to drive to the other side of town to look at what another supplier may be able to provide. Competitive product and pricing information is at our fingertips, and most internet businesses will happily deliver anywhere in the world. The competitive environment is becoming more intense, a trend which is likely to continue, and one which will lead many more businesses into difficult situations as a result of declining sales.

Declining sales can be a self-perpetuating event. A spiralling decline in sales is a common characteristic of businesses that have failed. As sales fall, cash inflows are reduced and the capacity of the business to replace stock or production inputs is subsequently restricted. A slow response to reducing overheads often causes continuing losses, further consuming assets of the business and restricting its capacity to fund stock purchases or production inputs. As stock and/or production levels decline, so the range and volume of product available to supply your customers is reduced, further impacting sales and leading to a downward spiral.

The deadly D's

At this point it would be remiss of me not to mention a group of seven events that almost invariably cause declining sales in SMEs. I refer to these events as the "deadly D's" – dependence, distraction, disputes, divorce, diversification, disease, and death. It is very common to see one or more of the deadly D's contributing to the pain being suffered by an SME that is in trouble. Even so, deadly D's are rarely anticipated and are, in most cases, poorly managed in terms of their impact on the business. The deadly D's have long been key contributors to business failure in SMEs.

DEPENDENCE

Customer dependence (otherwise known as "concentration risk") is a common characteristic of SMEs. Concentration risk arises when a business has one or just a few customers who represent the majority of the sales of the business. The dependent business relies both upon the continuing goodwill of its key customer/s, and upon the ongoing survival of its key customers, for its own survival. If it loses a key customer or one of its key customers fails, it is likely to fail itself. This occurs much more commonly than you might expect. Some large businesses encourage and exploit dependence, generally by awarding contracts to a much smaller business which then gears up to service the new contract (often funded by debt). The larger business then leverages off that dependence to secure reduced prices from the smaller business when the contract comes up for renewal. The smaller business then finds itself with no choice but to meet the price demands of its much larger customer, often at a high cost to its profit margins. Large retail chains are notorious for these tactics.

Supplier dependence arises where a business sources essential supplies from one or more critical suppliers which cannot be readily or quickly replaced. Supplier dependence can result in the business experiencing higher prices for purchases, stock outages, supply interruption, customer dissatisfaction, and possibly failure, if the key supplier refuses to supply or ceases to operate.

Industry dependence arises where the majority of the business's customers operate in the same industry and are, therefore, all exposed to the impacts of any downturn in that industry. This scenario is very common and most businesses are industry dependent. Some industries are more exposed to economic downturns (for example, mining and retail), while others are more vulnerable to weather extremes (farming, tourism). Political and policy changes can also cause major problems for industry-dependent firms. The car industry in Australia was decimated, and ultimately collapsed, as a result of the removal of tariffs on imported vehicles, which left locally-produced cars unable to compete with imported products. Suppliers to the car industry were left without their major customers and many collapsed.

There are other forms of dependence which pose varying levels of risk. In small and micro businesses, one such risk is key person dependence (where a business has one or a few critical employees).

Dependence is common and is not necessarily a fatal feature of a business, although it does expose the business to heightened risks. I have seen many businesses either suffer severe stress or fail as a result of issues related to dependence, such as the loss or cancellation of a critical contract, falling out with their major supplier, the failure of their major customer or a key supplier, or a serious downturn in the industry upon which they depend.

Wherever possible, dependence should be avoided by diversifying purchases, sales, and other dependency risks or, where diversification is not possible, by adopting measures to manage the impacts of any dependency event.

DISTRACTION

A distraction impedes the ability of management to focus on their role. It is a term that captures all the possible events that may divert management and leave a void in the business. Four of the following deadly D's (disputes, divorce, diversification, and disease) are examples of events that are a distraction for management, but the term "distraction" extends beyond these events to include anything that materially distracts management from their core role of managing the business. I have seen many examples in small businesses of key managers being distracted by personal issues, leading to serious impacts on the business. Legal action is another common, serious distraction encountered by businesses.

DISPUTES

Disputes are usually difficult to foresee and so it is difficult to prepare for them. Disputes can arise with a range of external parties including suppliers, customers, competitors, unions and, sometimes, government departments. Disputes can also, but less commonly, arise internally. Internally generated disputes include disputes with or between individual employees and disputes between the partners in a business. Partnerships are like marriages (indeed, the most common business partnership is between marital partners) and whenever two or more people are in a business relationship over an extended period of time there will invariably be disputes between them. In most cases, intractable disputes are resolved by one party buying out the other, although this introduces another avenue of common dispute in terms of the buyout price.

Disputes with suppliers or customers usually revolve around the performance of obligations or expectations, and can include failure to meet contracted timeframes, product/service quality problems, or pricing disagreements.

Disputes involving the partners in the business are likely to have a more immediate impact on the business, as they can quickly lead to decision paralysis and dysfunctional management. Most other disputes have a longer lead time before they escalate to the point of having a material impact on the business. This lead time usually allows time for a remedial strategy to be developed.

In most of the cases where I have seen disputes severely damage a business, there has been complacency on the part of one disputant and/or intransigence by one or both sides. Disputes that escalate to litigation rarely result in a benefit to either party. Court action has four negative characteristics – it is expensive, it is time consuming, it distracts managers from managing, and the outcome is always uncertain.

DIVORCE

Divorce (or separation) from a life partner is a very common cause of distraction for managers of small businesses and, typically, the most disruptive. This distraction often arises due to the stresses and strains placed on the relationship by the problems of the business. Many small businesses are started by one or both members of a relationship, and the ownership, and often the management, of the business is shared. Where the relationship subsequently sours, there is almost invariably acrimony and bitterness, which can fuel both personal and business disputes between the partners.

Where a business relationship is involved, it is most common for one partner to buy out the other from the business, and seek to reach a financial settlement with respect to the other assets of the relationship. Very few businesses have the cash available to fund the buyout of one partner by the other, and this often leads to circumstances where it is necessary for the partner who is assuming full ownership of the business to borrow money to acquire the other partner's interest. It is also typically the case that the servicing and repayment of that debt is sourced from the business, placing additional strain on the cash flow of the business without adding to the available working capital. The debt of a divorce settlement – indeed, any debt burden arising from a partnership dispute settlement – adds nothing to the business.

The physical and emotional impacts of a divorce can be equally debilitating to a business. Where both partners have previously been involved in the management of the business, there is a major void when one departs. In almost every case, an acrimonious divorce is a major distraction to management that, when combined with the financial burden of a divorce settlement, can place the business under serious threat.

DIVERSIFICATION

Diversification refers to circumstances where a business moves into an area of activity with which it is not familiar, generally with the intention of exploiting a perceived market opportunity or spreading risk across a range of business activities. Diversification is a risky action if it is not both well planned and well funded. I have seen many instances where diversification has had a serious adverse impact on an existing business. The reasons are quite simple – diversification means taking on unknown challenges, learning new skills and markets, incurring additional costs and, most importantly, distracting management from the core business while the new opportunity is established.

Diversification is not necessarily a bad thing if it is done with proper due diligence, proper resourcing (in particular, management resources and funding), proper timing, and on a scale that is readily manageable by the existing business.

DISEASE

Disease is an obvious cause of understandable distraction. The term and extent of the distraction is linked to the severity of the disease and the impacts of the disease on the individual manager. Disease is a difficult distraction to prevent or to manage, so it is necessary to have mitigation strategies in place to cover the impacts of a serious or sustained illness.

Disease on a wider scale, such as a pandemic, can also have a material impact on business sales as a result of shutdowns or other measures implemented to control the spread of infection. The timing of pandemics is impossible to predict. As demonstrated by the COVID-19 pandemic, the impacts on business trading can be severe and sustained, particularly in those industries that are directly impacted by infection control measures. SMEs are highly vulnerable to pandemics because they almost invariably lack the working capital and access to external funding necessary to weather a sustained downturn.

DEATH

Everybody dies and so every business runs the risk of being impacted by death. Yet, very few SMEs properly manage succession planning. The unexpected death of a key business manager is, not surprisingly, likely to be seriously disruptive to a business. As death is not generally predictable, it is another event that requires mitigation strategies, rather than preventative strategies, to be adopted.

Reducing profit margins

The profit margin of a business (usually referred to interchangeably as the "gross profit margin", "gross profit" or "gross margin") is the difference between sales and the direct input costs (labour and materials) that are related to the production and delivery of the products or services provided to the customer. For example, the gross profit of a furniture manufacturer is the value of a sale less the direct costs of producing and delivering the item of furniture that is sold (timber, fabric, other materials, production labour and delivery costs). Direct costs can be distinguished from overheads, which are costs that are necessary to run the business but are not directly related to the production of an individual product or the delivery of a specific service.

Businesses seeking to secure greater market share or new customers will often temporarily sacrifice gross margin to offer reduced sales prices. This is typically referred to as a "sale" and is very common in retailing. A temporary reduction in gross profit margin can also be a result of unplanned or unforeseen cost increases for direct inputs that cannot immediately be passed on to customers. In some cases, gross profit margins may be deliberately reduced for an extended period, or permanently, to secure a market position and deter new entrants from the industry. A reduction in gross margin can also be a function of poor control of direct costs.

However, a reduction in gross profit margin is most commonly caused by competitive pressures where it is necessary to reduce sales prices (and, therefore, gross profit margin) to maintain market share or retain customers in the face of price competition from competitors. In a competitive environment, increases in direct costs cannot always be passed on to customers. This means that gross margins can be eroded over time if the cost of direct inputs is growing at a faster rate than selling prices can increase. Accordingly, a reduction in gross margins is usually a strong indication of an increasingly competitive market environment. Contraction of gross margins caused by competitive pressures frequently leads to business failure. Strategies for addressing declining gross margins are discussed in Chapter 8.

Excessive overheads

Overheads are the costs incurred by businesses that are necessary for the operation of the business, but are not directly related to the product or service being supplied to a customer. Examples of overhead costs include premises rent, insurances, electricity and other utilities, marketing, cleaning, legal costs, administrative wages, and management salaries. Overhead expenses will be incurred whether or not a product is produced or a service is provided.

Overheads always represent a balancing act for management. On the one hand, overhead expenses facilitate the production of goods and services, so some level of overhead expenses cannot be avoided. On the other hand, overheads are a drag on profitability and need to be minimised. Inadequate resources can, on occasion, limit the capacity of a business to take advantage of growth opportunities. Excessive overheads can bring a business down.

There is no better example of this balancing act than the dilemma faced by management when it comes to deciding the amount of rented space they occupy. Do you take on just the amount of space required for the current level of business, or do you allow for some expansion by taking on a bit more space than you currently need? If so, how much extra space do you take on, bearing in mind that although the additional space is costing money, it will not provide any incremental contribution to the income of the business until such time as the business grows? Too much extra space will be a drag on the business. Too little extra space may impede taking on new growth opportunities, and you may have to move or split your business across more than one property to grow. However, if sales decline, you may be stuck paying rent on more space than you will need in the foreseeable future.

Importantly, the structure of the overhead costs of a business will have a material impact on whether or not the business can respond quickly to offset a fall in sales. A business with a high proportion of its overheads represented by fixed costs (costs that remain the same irrespective of the level of sales, such as premises rent and hire purchase charges) will inevitably be slow to adapt to declining sales and, in some cases, will be unable to respond by reducing overheads when sales fall. Businesses with a high proportion of overhead costs that can be quickly reduced will find it much easier to respond to declining sales.

Excessive overheads are generally found in established businesses that have experienced a decline in sales but have been unable or unwilling to reduce their overheads. Management often anticipates that the decline in sales is only temporary and the resources represented by the overheads will be required again in the near future. The managers of a business experiencing a decline in sales must make a judgement call in terms of balancing the retention of some excess capacity to meet future growth opportunities against the overhead costs relating to the excess capacity.

Reducing overheads often involves difficult decisions such as making staff redundant, selling off unutilised or under-utilised plant and equipment, or reducing purchases from longstanding suppliers. It has been my experience that, more often than not, managers will avoid or defer these difficult decisions and take the line of least resistance (either out of loyalty or fear) by not taking urgent action to reduce overheads. If overheads remain high as sales decline, the profitability of a business can rapidly be eroded and trading losses can result.

Businesses with excessive overheads are often referred to as being "fat", meaning they are carrying excess costs that are not essential to the business, or costs that could be reduced by carrying out some functions of the business more efficiently. Businesses that have a relatively low level of overheads are generally referred to as being "lean".

Identifying, and methods of reducing, excessive overheads are discussed in Chapter 8.

If the causes of your trading losses are not obvious to you, one easy way of identifying the potential causes is to compare the changes in your profit and loss account over the past two or three years on an item-by-item basis. You should be able to readily identify material changes that have impacted upon the profitability of the business from year to year, although it is more difficult if all of the years you are comparing are years in which the business made losses. Of course, the reliability of the information that you will get from this comparison is only as good as the reliability of the accounts themselves. I recall a transport business with a junior accountant who was not including depreciation in the management accounts. The owners of the business, who did not closely review the accounts, thought they were making profits when, in fact, they were making substantial losses.

Non-trading (extraordinary) losses

There are other non-trading events that can result in a business incurring losses. Such an event would be considered an "extraordinary event" and the losses resulting would be treated as extraordinary losses rather than trading losses. Most of these types of events will cause temporary disruption that will not be fatal to a business that has a reasonable level of equity capital. On occasion, the impacts are very serious, as demonstrated by the following examples. Sometimes the impacts are so severe they cause a business to fail or be weakened to the point where it may fall prey to threats, such as adversarial actions by competitors and economic downturn.

There have been some spectacular, well-publicised extraordinary losses incurred by major corporations over the years. Perhaps the largest of these were the losses incurred by BP as a result of the Deepwater Horizon oil spillage into the Gulf of Mexico in 2010, which is reported to have cost BP more than $50 billion, including almost $19 billion to settle claims by US state and federal departments. Some other examples of major extraordinary losses include:

- the Exxon Valdez oil spillage into Alaska's Prince William Sound in 1989
- Volkswagen's recall and refit of up to 11 million cars following the diesel emissions scandal (where vehicles were fitted with software designed to defeat emissions testing)
- billions in restoration costs and up to $7 billion in fines payable by BHP Billiton and its partner Vale after a mine tailings dam burst in Brazil in early 2016, causing substantial environmental damage.

Events giving rise to extraordinary losses are also seen on a much smaller scale and in different forms, including when:

- an asset of the business is sold for less than its written down value due to a weak market
- when stock is unexpectedly damaged (such as by a storm or fire) or stolen
- accidents occur, giving rise to business disruption

- legal disputes arise with competitors, suppliers, customers, environmentalists or government authorities
- fraud is perpetrated upon the business (usually by staff)
- natural disasters strike (floods, hurricanes, earthquakes, tsunamis, forest fires)
- product defects result in product recalls, products having to be withdrawn from the market, and/or prosecution.

As the name implies, the events that give rise to extraordinary losses are almost always unforeseen (although not always unforeseeable). As these events are difficult to predict, it is only possible to seek to avoid them, to be prepared to respond to them when they occur, and to mitigate their potential impacts if they occur. In Chapter 8 we will look at how to mitigate the threat of extraordinary losses arising from such events.

Poor working capital management

Cash is king. Many profitable businesses have run out of cash and gone broke. Profits are ultimately only beneficial to your business if you turn those profits into cash. Consider a profitable sale to a customer on credit. At the time of the sale, a profit is recorded in the books. However, if your customer doesn't pay your invoice, then the profit on that sale will vaporise and turn into a loss – you will not only lose the profit on the sale, you will also lose all of the money you invested in making the products or services that went into the sale.

"Working capital" is made up of the assets available to a business to meet its short-term obligations. It is the sum of the resources available to the business that can be converted to cash so the business can pay its costs, less the current cash obligations of the business. This equates to the capacity of the business to fund its current operations. Mathematically, working capital is the sum of the current assets of the business (typically comprising cash, marketable securities, stock, and debtors) less the current liabilities of the business (typically made up of creditors, employee entitlements, and short-term loan repayments due).

The relationship between current assets and current liabilities is often measured as a "working capital ratio" where current assets are divided by current liabilities. A ratio greater than one indicates a "positive" working capital position (meaning the business has enough current assets to meet its short-term liabilities and to fund its current level of operations). A ratio less than one indicates that short-term liabilities exceed the assets available to meet those obligations, resulting in a "negative" working capital position (indicating that the business has insufficient working capital to fund its current level of operations).

Overtrading

Overtrading is a term used to describe circumstances where a business is trading at an unsustainable level. It is an extreme example of poor working capital management. What differentiates overtrading from other working capital management issues is that it generally arises in profitable businesses experiencing rapid growth. Often, these businesses are new or young businesses in dynamic growth industries, or with new, innovative products where the depth of the market is untested. Overtrading can also occur when an established business experiences rapid expansion, such as when it secures a new, large contract or starts producing a new product line.

Overtrading occurs when a business trades with insufficient working capital to fund its rapid growth. It can result in severe cash stress which, inevitably, leads to problems with payment of staff, creditors, debt payments, and taxation debts. The consequences of overtrading can be fatal, although more commonly the business is forced to raise equity funding at a substantial discount to the real value of the business; or the business is sold off at a bargain price.

So, how does overtrading occur? Managers who are given the opportunity to take on new orders or contracts rarely turn them away. In doing so they often fail to assess the amount of capital required to fund them. This is particularly the case when the business is on a very strong growth trajectory and management are distracted by a raft of new business opportunities and issues arising from this growth.

Every business incurs costs in supplying goods and/or services to its customers, and every new order or contract requires additional costs to be incurred by the business. Where those new orders or contracts are flowing in thick and fast, it can be difficult to measure the incremental working capital requirements of the business in advance of accepting the order or contract. It is often the case that management only catches up with the funding requirements of the business when the business has exhausted its working capital and there is suddenly pressure to come up with additional funding. Young businesses without an established track record do not always have ready access to undrawn bank funding lines, so they are forced to resort to equity funding which can come at a very high price when urgency is involved.

The trading cycle

In order to understand how poor working capital management can lead to the downfall of the business, it is necessary to consider how businesses function and how they fund their business activities.

Every business has what is known as a "trading cycle". The business starts out with cash (or credit which is convertible to cash) which it uses to acquire resources, such as labour, raw materials, produce, equipment, and premises. These resources are combined in some way to produce products and/or services that are sold to customers. Upon delivery or completion of the work, the customer is charged for the products or services provided. When the customer pays, the business is again possessed of cash (hopefully more cash than it started with) and the cycle begins again. This process is known as the trading cycle of the business.

During the trading cycle there are regular changes in the assets and liabilities of the business. In a manufacturing business, for example, cash is used to purchase raw materials and labour, which are processed into a product, which then becomes trading stock, which is, in turn, sold to a customer, creating a debt due from the customer which, when paid, is then turned back into cash. The trading cycle of a manufacturer is illustrated in the following diagram.

DEBTOR

CASH

RAW MATERIALS

SALES

DIAGRAM 1
THE TRADING CYCLE
(Manufacturer)

FINISHED GOODS (STOCK)

WORK IN PROGRESS

Each step of the trading cycle requires that there are adequate resources available to complete the step. For example, if there are insufficient funds to purchase the raw materials, no product can be produced. A business is particularly vulnerable in the stage where a debt is owed to the business by its customer (debtor) because the business has no control (and generally no visibility) over the resources (and goodwill) of the customer. Recouping the debt owed requires that your customer has both the capacity and the willingness to pay you.

Each stage of the trading cycle also requires time. Time is required to secure the resources necessary to produce your product or service – whether it is to acquire trading stock for a retailer, raw materials for a manufacturer, or labour for a service provider, there will be a time delay between making a decision to acquire those resources and the availability of those resources. Businesses that combine these resources to manufacture a product or develop a service, or otherwise add value before selling, will encounter a further time delay in turning the raw materials into a finished product. In the case of businesses that hold stock, there is also a time delay between purchase or production of that stock and selling it. Businesses that sell on credit additionally have a time lag after they sell their product while they wait to be paid. The length of the trading cycle will vary from business to business. In some cases, the trading cycle may only be measured in terms of minutes (for example a taxi owner-driver who delivers a service to his customers over a period of a few minutes and receives immediate payment) whereas, for others, the trading cycle will be measured in months, possibly years. Consider the trading cycle of a developer who buys land and develops high-rise apartments or an office tower on the land. The developer's trading cycle could well be measured over many years.

Whatever the length of the trading cycle, time is money for every business. All other things being equal, the faster a business can complete its trading cycle the less capital it will require, the less debt it will carry, and the lower its capital and debt costs will become. This means it will be able to offer lower prices to its customers than competitors with a longer trading cycle.

There are other elements of the trading cycle that can have impacts on the time it takes for a business to complete its trading cycle. Examples of these time-sensitive trading cycle elements include:

- the time it takes for delivery of raw materials or stock from your supplier or wholesaler after you order them
- the time it takes to convert raw materials into a finished product (the equivalent of which in a service business might be the time it takes to complete the delivery of the service being provided to the customer)
- the time that finished products or stock are held by your business before they are sold
- the time taken to deliver products to your customers
- how quickly (or slowly) your customer pays you.

Think about the trading cycle of your business and work out how long each element of your trading cycle takes to be completed. Identify areas where the trading cycle of your business can be shortened.

Businesses can (and do) use various techniques and strategies to minimise the length of the trading cycle. "Just-in-time" purchasing, manufacturing and stock management, which is designed to produce stock just before it is required by the customer, is one example of a process commonly used by businesses to reduce the length of their trading cycle.

How the trading cycle affects working capital

Changes to the trading cycle of a business have a direct impact on the working capital of the business. Shortening your trading cycle can reduce the amount of working capital required to fund your business. Conversely, a longer trading cycle will require more funding. This is a logical conclusion, given that higher time-related costs such as overheads and debt interest will be incurred over the longer trading cycle. Businesses within the same industry that have a shorter trading cycle than their competitors will, all other things being equal, have lower costs than their competitors. Businesses that allow their trading cycle to be stretched will not only have higher cost structures, they will also expose themselves to unnecessary risks, and, potentially, have unnecessary cash stress.

The following simple example demonstrates how the timing of the trading cycle can have a big impact upon the amount of working capital funding required by a business.

EXAMPLE – JACK'S FURNITURE

Jack has established a new business called Jack's Furniture that manufactures and sells high-end handmade tables. It takes Jack's small factory one month to make ten tables. Jack spends $50,000 each month in production costs. Jack's only customer is a boutique furniture retail chain that buys all of Jack's tables and pays him at the end of the month following delivery. To keep it simple, let's assume that when he first starts out, Jack has no suppliers willing to extend him credit, so he needs cash to buy materials, employ labour, and rent premises. These inputs are then turned into his first ten tables, which become Jack's trading stock. To produce his first ten tables, Jack needs to have cash of $50,000. Since Jack knows he won't be paid for a month after he delivers his first tables to his customer, Jack needs enough cash to make tables for two months, or $100,000.

To illustrate the changes in the working capital in Jack's business, we will use a table at each step. In the first table below Jack starts off with working capital of $100,000, which is all in cash.

Jack's Furniture	Month 1
At the beginning of the month	
Cash	$100,000
Stock of unsold tables at cost	$—
Debtors owing to Jack	$—
Total working capital	**$100,000**

Over the course of the first month, Jack spends $50,000 making ten tables. He now has $50,000 in cash and 10 tables in stock that have cost him $50,000.

Jack's Furniture	Month 1
Just before delivery of the tables	
Cash	$50,000
Stock of unsold tables at cost	$50,000
Debtors owing to Jack	$—
Total working capital	**$100,000**

Note that Jack's working capital is now made up of $50,000 in cash and $50,000 in his stock of unsold tables.

Jack then delivers the ten tables to his customer on the last day of the month. He invoices his customer $6,000 per table ($60,000 in total). Jack no longer has any tables in stock and his working capital is now represented by the $50,000 he has in cash, plus the $60,000 owed to him by his customer (a "debtor" because he owes Jack money).

Jack's Furniture	Month 1
Just before delivery of the tables	
Cash	$50,000
Stock of unsold tables at cost	$—
Debtors	$60,000
Total working capital	**$110,000**

Note that Jack's working capital has increased by $10,000, representing the profit margin added to the cost of the tables when he sold them to his customer.

At this time, Jack's working capital has been increased by the $10,000 profit on the first batch of tables – but he hasn't yet received any cash from his customer (who has agreed to pay Jack 30 days after invoice date). While Jack is waiting to be paid by his customer, he uses his remaining $50,000 in cash to make ten more tables.

In month 2, Jack makes another ten tables (at a cost of $50,000).

Jack's Furniture	Month 2
Just before delivery of the tables	
Cash	$—
Stock of unsold tables at cost	$50,000
Debtors	$60,000
Total working capital	**$110,000**

Near the end of the second month, after completing the second batch of tables, Jack's working capital is represented by stock of ten tables awaiting delivery to his customer and the debt of $60,000 owed by his customer for the tables he delivered in month 1.

On the last day of the second month Jack delivers and invoices the second batch of tables for a further $60,000. On the same day, Jack gets paid by his customer for the first invoice. Jack now has $60,000 in cash and a debt of $60,000 owed by his customer.

Jack's Furniture	Month 2
On the last day of the month	
Cash	$60,000
Stock of unsold tables at cost	$—
Debtors	$60,000
Total working capital	**$120,000**

By the end of the second month, the working capital in his business has grown from $100,000 to $120,000 as a result of profit.

The cash he receives is used to produce more tables and the trading cycle begins again.

Now consider a scenario where Jack's customer decides that instead of paying Jack at the end of the month following delivery (30 days) it is going to pay Jack 60 days (two months) after the tables are delivered. That change in payment terms means it will now be three months from the time Jack starts producing tables until he receives his first payment from his customer. Jack will now need to fund three months of production costs before he gets paid. Jack's trading cycle has been extended by one month and Jack has to pay out $150,000 in production costs before he gets paid, instead of $100,000. That means Jack has to come up with an extra $50,000 in working capital for his business, just because his customer pays him more slowly. Assuming Jack had to borrow that money, he would have to pay interest on an extra $50,000 in debt which would reduce his profits. Jack has done nothing differently, but his trading cycle has been extended by the actions of his customer. As a result, the working capital Jack is required to source for his business is $50,000 higher, and his costs have been increased by interest.

Extended payment by customers is a very common occurrence in business, particularly in times of economic slowdowns. Businesses (often large businesses) will vary their trading terms by increasing the amount of time they take to pay their suppliers in order to conserve cash in their own business. There is often a high degree of dependency upon these large businesses, which makes it very difficult for the smaller businesses to walk away from the large business. The bargaining power of a small business is usually such that they are not in a position to reject the change in payment terms. In the example above, Jack has only one customer. He is totally dependent upon them to buy his tables, and vulnerable to any change in payment terms they may impose upon him.

As the example of Jack's business demonstrates, changes to the timing of the trading cycle can have material impacts on the amount of working capital required by a business. These impacts are often not well understood (particularly by SMEs) and very commonly lead to unforeseen cash flow stress in businesses. Extending the trading cycle of a business adds to the amount of working capital required by the business. Conversely, reducing the length of the trading cycle will reduce the amount of working capital required by the business. This is an important concept to understand, as managing the trading cycle can play an important role in a turnaround strategy.

Working capital is also a measure of the robustness (or vulnerability) of the business. A business with a positive working capital position (that is, where the current assets exceed the short-term financial obligations) has the capacity to fund the trading activities of the business without the need for external support (provided that the working capital position is effectively managed). A business with a significant excess of current assets over current liabilities has the capacity to expand its operating activities without external funding. On the other hand, a business with a negative working capital position (a position where short-term obligations exceed the current assets available to meet those obligations) faces the prospect of cash stress, as it does not have the capacity to generate sufficient cash internally (in the short term) to fund its operating requirements. Such a business requires either an injection of external funds or very astute working capital management, or both, to avoid serious difficulties. A negative working capital position is a very common feature of businesses experiencing serious problems.

Many businesses in decline experience a deteriorating working capital ratio over time. This can be a very good leading indicator of a deterioration in the financial strength of the business. Regular monitoring of your working capital ratio can provide you with one simple and quick indicator of the health of your business, although working capital must not be viewed in isolation as the only indicator of the health of your business.

Sustaining a positive working capital position requires effective management. Allowing the trading cycle to be extended by poor management of one or more of the stages of the cycle will result in an increase in the working capital requirements of the business, and potentially change a positive working capital position to a negative one. This outcome results from the additional liabilities that are incurred due to the delays in the trading cycle. Conversely, efficient management of the timing of each element of the trading cycle will reduce the working capital requirements of the business, facilitate cost efficiencies, and improve capacity for growth without the need for external support.

The cash cycle

The trading cycle is all about cycling cash back into cash via the trading cycle and, hopefully (by virtue of profitable trading), increasing the amount of cash available at the end of each cycle. This rotating flow of money via the trading cycle is referred to as the "cash cycle". Ultimately, the time it takes for cash to return to cash in the business through the trading cycle (the cash cycle) is the measure that can have a critical impact on the business.

Cash lock-up

Cash is the ultimate currency in business, as it is used to meet the liabilities of the business as and when they fall due. It is, therefore, critical to release cash into the business as a priority means of avoiding some of the most serious threats to the business. Cash "lock-up" occurs when cash is invested during the trading cycle in business inputs, trading stock or debtors for extended periods of time. Cash lock-up extends the trading cycle and most commonly occurs where a business carries excess inventory or obsolete trading stock. It can also occur when businesses are tardy in collecting debts owed to the business by customers or when key customers change trading terms to slow down payment to the business.

The most extreme form of cash lock-up is where customers who have been supplied on credit don't pay at all. In these circumstances, it is usually necessary to pursue legal avenues of recovery and extended timeframes arise (if the business gets paid at all). The business has invested significant money in supplying goods or services to those customers, which is now at risk. For most businesses, such a catastrophic event would cause a disruption to cash flow that is so significant it may cause the business to fail.

Cash is king

The point to note here is that making a profitable sale doesn't mean much until the sale is converted into cash. If the sale isn't converted into cash, not only does the profit evaporate but so does all of the money you have sunk into the products or services that went into making the sale. Over the years I have seen many businesses fail because their customers failed to pay them. Success in business – indeed, survival in business – is dependent upon turning sales into cash. For this reason, your mindset should be that your profits are not realised until such time as you have turned them into cash.

Almost every business that fails will experience a cash flow crisis along the way. Cash shortages are by far the most common symptom of businesses that fail. It stands to reason, therefore, that cash is the most important element of working capital. The ultimate objective of every manager must be to generate profits and turn those profits into cash.

Lack of equity/excessive debt

Lack of equity is not, of itself, a cause of business failure but it often results in the premature or unnecessary failure of businesses. It deserves to be noted as a major contributor to the failure of businesses.

There are only two sources of funds for a business – equity and debt. Every business is funded by a combination of funds provided by the owners of the business (comprising funds directly contributed to the business in the form of capital and accumulated profits) and funds provided by others (banks, other financiers, and creditors). The funding provided by the owners of a business is referred to as "equity" (or sometimes "equity capital" or "capital"). The funding provided by others is known as "debt".

Equity is characterised by the absence of an obligation or timeframe to repay the money to the provider of the equity and by the absence of a guaranteed price/return on the equity provided. When a business collapses, equity funding comes last in the hierarchy of payment priorities. Everyone else owed money by the business gets paid before the owners of the business if the business is wound up.

Debt is funding provided to the business by third parties. Typically, debt has a fixed term for repayment and incurs a known price (generally made up of interest and fees). Debt generally enjoys some form of security and has priority over equity in terms of repayment in a winding up. Debt providers also enjoy contractual and statutory rights to enforce the repayment of their debts.

As there is no specific repayment obligation, equity is "patient" funding. Equity imparts resilience to a business because it provides the capacity for a business to carry trading losses for a period of time and/or to fund capital expenditure to restructure or improve a business. Equity also provides a capacity for a business to fund its growth. When a business experiences difficult trading conditions, lack of equity increases cash flow stress. In these circumstances, the funding needs of the business are usually met by increasing debt, either by borrowing more or by stretching out payments to creditors and taxation authorities. If equity is deficient, debt increases, and so do the risks to the business.

Very few small or medium businesses are established with adequate equity funding. Usually this is because the owners simply don't have the equity to contribute, cannot raise outside equity, or do not wish to give up ownership or control of the business to outsiders. In addition, equity is more expensive than debt (as the providers of equity funding require a higher return to compensate for the additional risks they take) so business owners prefer to use debt to fund their business. As businesses grow, the owners are often reluctant (or unable) to contribute further equity, or reluctant to sell down their interest in the business by introducing outside equity investors. Most small and medium businesses seek to fund their growth with debt, and grow the equity in the business organically (that is, by growing equity over time via debt-funded profits).

When a business gets into trouble, it is (or will be) typically unable to meet all of its financial obligations in a timely manner. Where a business has adequate equity, it is able to better withstand downturns in trading or cash flow. However, attracting equity investors to a business that is experiencing serious troubles is extremely difficult, due to the increased risk of losing money. As a result, even if new equity could be attracted, it would come at a very high price – making it even less attractive for the current owners to introduce new equity to the business, despite what may be a critical need.

The equity in the business provides the capacity to fund trading losses and capital expenditures through a turnaround process. Lack of equity restricts the quantum of losses that a business can incur before it becomes insolvent. This often dictates the length of time a business can spend working through a turnaround. Most SMEs have low levels of equity, and so they are poorly positioned to cope with an extended period of financial stress or a protracted turnaround.

Sometimes no amount of equity will ultimately save the business. However, many businesses that have the potential to survive are unable to withstand the impacts of short-term losses or cash stress because of a lack of equity, ultimately leading to their failure.

Ineffective management

Management are charged with responsibility for effectively managing the operations of any business. Those responsibilities extend to strategic planning, financial control, cost management, sales and marketing, people management, and managing the resources of the business. It is difficult to escape the conclusion that management makes a significant contribution to a business failure.

The failure of any business is ultimately a result of one or more of:

- not being adequately prepared for events or circumstances that might put its survival at risk
- failing to respond in a timely manner to events or circumstances that place the business at risk (such as when the response of the business is too slow or ineffective)
- the lack of financial capacity to withstand the impact of the events or circumstances that are placing the survival of the business at risk.

All of these factors are management failures. Usually, the failure of management to respond to problems, or the inadequacy of the response, can be attributed to at least one of the following three reasons:

- Failure to acknowledge that there is a problem until it is too late (denial is often a result of not knowing what to do about the problem).
- Assuming that the problem is temporary and will rectify itself without the need for any action.
- Failure to identify and respond to the cause of the problem in a timely manner.

In my experience, there have been many instances where an earlier acknowledgement and understanding of the problems confronting the business could well have resulted in the business being saved from failure. Whatever the reason, the lack of a decisive and timely response from management to the problems being experienced by a business can have fatal consequences.

Businesses sometimes experience serious problems because of strategic errors made by management. Some of these errors include diversification into unfamiliar industries, taking on projects that are too big (overtrading) or too complex for the business, failure to adequately assess project risks or costs, and paying too much when acquiring assets or businesses. Every manager makes strategic decisions (hopefully based on the best available information) and, on occasion, these decisions will prove to be wrong. These errors can result in difficulties being experienced by the business and it is management's response to those difficulties that will ultimately decide the fate of the business. Strategic decisions can, in some cases, lead to business failures.

There are obvious lessons for management when a business is experiencing serious difficulties. It is a period when reflection on management practices and skills is appropriate and necessary as part of the turnaround process.

2. The characteristics of a failing business

Abusiness that is not doing well will begin to show symptoms that progressively get worse. Treating the symptoms will alleviate the immediate effects, but the problems will never be cured unless the underlying cause is located and removed.

Warning signs (symptoms)

In the previous chapter we looked at the causes of business failure. There are warning signs that signal that a business is experiencing problems. These symptoms, left untreated, could result in the failure of the business.

A person with the common cold will experience headaches, a sore throat, sneezing and coughing. These are not the cause of the cold – they are merely symptoms of the cold. While it is necessary to treat the symptoms to alleviate the physical distress caused by the cold, treating the symptoms will not cure the virus that is causing the cold. Similarly, a business experiencing problems will exhibit symptoms and these symptoms need to be recognised and treated early to reduce the threat they represent to the business. Until the cause of the symptoms is identified and remedied, the symptoms will continue or recur.

The three most common symptoms of a troubled business are falling sales, declining profits/trading losses, and declining gross profit margins. These are important early warning signs and they are typically found together. Declining sales is by far the most common and easy-to-recognise early warning sign. It is also generally the most reliable sign that a business is heading towards failure, particularly where a downward sales trend becomes evident. Declining profitability may manifest itself in the form of a decline in the operating profit of the business, or as reduced gross profit margins. Declining gross profit margins are not always tied to a fall in sales, but they generally evidence a need to reduce margins to preserve sales in an increasingly competitive market. Where sales and gross profit margins are stable but operating profit is declining, the cause is invariably an upward shift in the overheads of the business.

Generally, a business in decline will move through a process that can be divided broadly into stages. The early symptoms are most commonly those just described. As the health of a business deteriorates, other symptoms begin to emerge. Cash stress, overdue creditors, unpaid taxes, declining stock levels and increasing bank debt are extremely common symptoms of a business in the more advanced stages of decline.

In some circumstances, cash stress may become evident and be quite an early warning sign. One situation where cash stress can become evident early is where a business has few customers and a key customer is unable (or unwilling) to pay monies owed to the business. Another such situation is when a business is overtrading. These are examples where the symptoms of distress emerge very quickly. However, cash stress is not always evident as an early warning sign because, in most cases, cash stress will be deferred by the use of various alternative actions to preserve cash, such as delaying payments to creditors.

Delaying the payment of creditors is one of the most common and easiest actions that management can take when the early stages of cash stress begin to emerge. This will result in an increase in the average age of creditors (the average number of days for payment of trade creditors' accounts). Very slow payment may result in supply or credit being stopped, suppliers placing the business on cash on delivery (COD) terms, and payment demands being made by creditors.

One of the largest creditors of most businesses is the taxation authority. Since taxes are not essential to continued trading, and the revenue authorities are usually slow to take action, it is very common for taxes to be overdue in a declining business.

As the decline of a business progresses and suppliers impose restrictions on supply, or cash payment terms, the business will begin to be slow to replace stock, resulting in declining stock levels and stock outages becoming more common.

Another common symptom of trouble will be an increase in bank debt. As cash from trading becomes inadequate to meet the requirements of the business, credit lines will be drawn down and/or new credit lines will be established to provide supplemental funding to the business.

Although these examples do not represent all of the symptoms that might be experienced by a business in difficulty, they are by far the most common and will be seen in the vast majority of cases.

The following table sets out some of the typical symptoms that you will notice as a business moves through the stages of decline.

Typical symptoms of a business in decline		
Early stages	**Middle stages**	**Final stages**
Sales decline	Trend of declining sales and profits becomes evident	History of trading losses develops
Gross profit margins reducing	Bank debt increasing	Breach of bank loan terms
Overheads rising as a share of income	Insufficient cash to make normal payment of suppliers and other creditors	Inadequate stock to maintain sales
Operating profit declines/ trading losses	Stock levels not replenished	Key staff leaving
Late lodgement of tax forms and slow payment of tax obligations	Tax arrears/payment arrangements with the taxation authority	Taxation authority debt repayment arrangements breached
Cash a bit tight from time to time	Cash regularly tight, especially midmonth	Serious and continuing cash stress
Creditor balances increasing	Creditors calling and threatening action. COD required by suppliers	Legal correspondence or statutory demands issued

In many cases the symptoms of trouble are (at least initially) over-looked, ignored or expected to remedy themselves. These symptoms require action without which the impacts of the risk events are likely to escalate and ultimately be damaging, if not fatal, to the business. In the vast majority of cases the impacts of the symptoms can be effectively managed.

Managers of businesses experiencing problems often focus their attention exclusively on the treatment of the symptoms of decline. They mistake the symptoms for the causes and mistakenly believe that treating the symptoms will remove the cause or causes of the problems. It is important that you do not make this mistake. While responding to, and treating, the symptoms may be necessary to keep the business alive, it is essential that the underlying causes be identified and remedied if a successful turnaround is to be achieved and business failure is to be avoided.

The stages of decline

Business failure is rarely an overnight event. Most businesses that fail go through a lengthy period of decline before ultimately meeting their demise. The events leading up to the ultimate failure of a business usually take time to work their destructive forces upon the business. As a result, businesses experiencing a downturn go through a series of steps on the way down, through a pattern of changes that is fairly common to all businesses in problem situations (other than those arising from a catastrophic event) as illustrated in the following diagram:

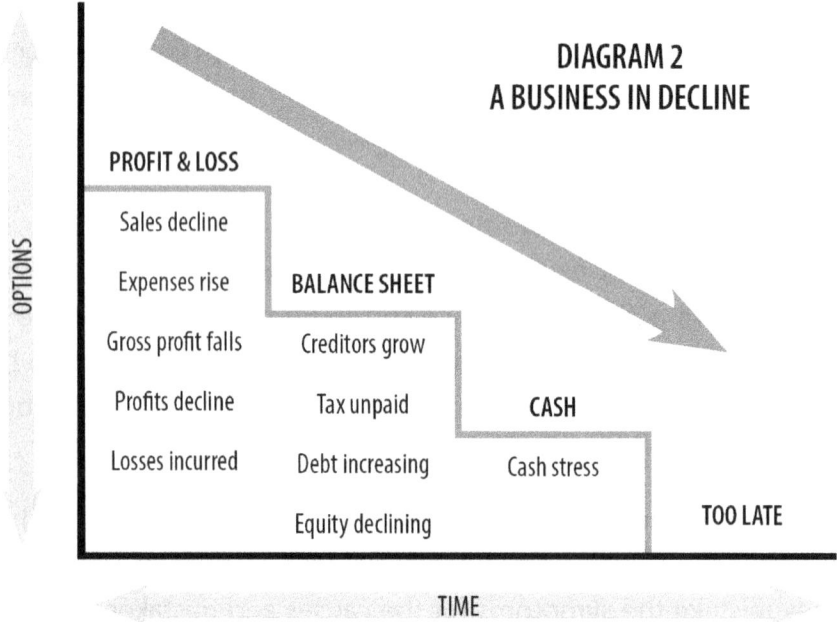

**DIAGRAM 2
A BUSINESS IN DECLINE**

OPTIONS

PROFIT & LOSS

Sales decline

Expenses rise   **BALANCE SHEET**

Gross profit falls   Creditors grow

Profits decline   Tax unpaid   **CASH**

Losses incurred   Debt increasing   Cash stress

Equity declining   **TOO LATE**

TIME

The most important take away from this graphic is the message that it is important to recognise and respond early and decisively to the symptoms of a business in decline. As the business moves through the stages of decline, the problems confronting the business become more serious and more difficult to remedy. The longer the decline continues, the more difficult it will become to secure the time required to resolve the problems, and the greater the likelihood of action being taken by others that will result in the failure of the business.

In my experience, managers often don't begin to try to turn the business around until it has reached the point of a cash crisis. On many occasions that is simply too late. The slow response, or failure to respond, by managers to symptoms of trouble is often cited as the most common reason why a business cannot be successfully turned around.

As Diagram 2 illustrates, the earlier action is taken, the more strategy options are available to resolve the problems causing the decline in the business; and the more time is available to implement those strategies to turn the business around. Never make the mistake of believing that a problem will correct itself.

Movement down through the various stages of decline can, and often does, take years. A downturn in any business generally has its origins in a decline in the profitability of the business and so the earliest warning signs of a downturn in the business are to be found in the elements of the business that contribute to the profit and loss account – sales, gross profit margin, and expenses. Unfavourable changes in one or more of these elements (all other things remaining equal) will contribute to a decline in profit. If these unfavourable changes persist then, over time, there will be a deterioration of elements of the business that are to be found on the balance sheet – outstanding creditors' balances grow above normal levels, debt increases, taxes remain unpaid, and trading losses consume the equity in the business. These changes are driven by declining trading outcomes and will be more pronounced in businesses where losses are being incurred. The impacts will be slower in businesses where profitability is declining but not yet to the point of making losses. The final step in the demise of the business will be a cash crisis which will arise when the capacity to fund the business from the balance sheet (creditors, debt and unpaid taxes) has been exhausted.

There is no sharp delineation between the various stages of decline and symptoms will overlap. There is no specific norm or standard when it comes to the stages of decline, and no specific timeframe. I have seen some businesses collapse in a matter of weeks and yet, in other cases, I have seen them last for many years.

3. Eight rules for a successful turnaround

Before we go into detail about the turnaround process, I want to touch on eight principles or rules that you should use for guidance throughout the turnaround process. If you like, these are the overarching policies and practices you should apply to ensure you maintain your focus on the things that are important. You should use these rules when reviewing and assessing your forward strategies and in making decisions where there are conflicting interests and opportunities available. Of course, you can never anticipate everything that might happen, but by following these rules you will be able to respond effectively and quickly to unforeseen events.

Rule No. 1 – Concentrate on cash, count every dollar, and make every dollar count

Whatever else may be important in turning around your business, the most important objective in the turnaround process will be to maintain a focus on generating and conserving cash. The reason the vast majority of businesses fail is because they simply run out of cash. Many businesses that have been working through turnaround plans have failed because they ran out of money before their plan could be implemented or completed. They failed to appreciate the amount of cash they would need to maintain their business through the turnaround process, and failed to determine where those funds were coming from. *Always keep cash in mind*. Always have a cash plan so that you know how much cash you have to play with, where it is coming from and where it is going. *Make sure that every dollar you spend has to be spent* and that every dollar you earn is collected as quickly as possible. Make cash flow your number one priority, and keep it at the top of your priority list throughout the turnaround process.

Rule No. 2 – Stabilise, and maintain stability

Your business is in difficulty. There will be a number of threats facing the business. These threats might include loss of credit terms with suppliers; difficulty securing money to pay bills or wages for staff; overdue tax payments; threats of wind-up action from creditors; and threats of action from your financier due to late or missed loan payments. These are all common symptoms of a business that is in trouble, and just a few of the possible problems you may be facing. Some of these issues will be potentially fatal to the business if they are not carefully and continually managed. Do not turn a blind eye to these issues. You need to identify and manage these issues (and keep managing them) to remove any immediate threat to the business if you are to get the chance to implement your turnaround strategy. Restoring and maintaining stability must be a key priority and a guiding principle of the turnaround process.

Rule No. 3 – Organise, plan and prioritise

Turning your business around will involve a number of steps and actions that will need to be well organised and planned. There is a raft of issues to be considered and there will be a large number of action items to be completed; all of which must be coordinated and managed to achieve the ultimate objective of turning the business around. You will be inundated with problems that need to be resolved. Pressures will come from all directions at once, and it will be necessary to allocate resources to priority issues. Good organisation and planning will help you to avoid being distracted by the "squeakiest wheel". You will need to organise, plan, and prioritise all of these elements if you are to stabilise your business, and maintain stability during the turnaround process.

A successful turnaround process must begin with the preparation of a plan. In order to prepare a plan, you will need to identify and understand the problems that need to be resolved (both symptoms and causes of the problems will need to be considered), develop strategies to resolve those problems, identify the resources you will need to implement your strategies, and put all that into a prioritised timeline.

A turnaround plan will provide clear guidance on what is to be done, how it is to be done, when it is to be done, and by whom it is to be done. Your strategy plan should include a reference point to measure the extent to which the plan has been successfully implemented. Preparing a turnaround plan at the outset will also give you the opportunity to assess whether, and how, a successful turnaround can be achieved.

Rule No. 4 – Time is critical

As illustrated by Diagram 2 (p 44) the longer you wait to take steps to address the symptoms and causes of problems in your business, the fewer the options and opportunities that are available to address the problems, and the greater the risk that an external party will take action that may cause the business to fail. The message here is that you should never ignore the symptoms or expect them to go away on their own. Do not assume that the symptoms being experienced by your business are temporary or that the market will ultimately come back to where it was before. I have seen many businesses fail while the managers have waited for the markets to return to their previous level, either in terms of volumes or prices. This characteristic is commonly seen in smaller property developers who are usually reluctant to acknowledge downward movements in the market or to sell stock at a price below their last sale or their price expectations. More often than not, they will wait out the market in anticipation of an upturn to previous levels – and a lot will go broke while they wait.

The longer you wait, the harder it will be to turn your business around and the fewer strategy options you will have. Be proactive at the outset and throughout the turnaround process. Get on the front foot and stay there. Act immediately upon any threats to your business that may have serious and/or continuing adverse impacts. Never assume that someone will give you more time to make a payment, comply with a contractual obligation or respond to a threat.

Rule No. 5 – Communicate thoughtfully, effectively and regularly

One of the most common characteristics that I have seen in businesses that have been successfully turned around is the ability of management to communicate. There are many stakeholders with an interest in the success of your business beyond yourself. There are employees whose jobs may be affected, creditors whose debts may be at risk, customers who rely on your products for their own success, lenders to your business and, of course, shareholders. It is highly likely that you will rely on the support of many of these stakeholders to achieve a successful turnaround. In most cases you will be asking stakeholders to provide your business with favourable terms or additional support or forbearance. Securing that support will largely depend upon the relationship you have, and that you are able to maintain, with the relevant stakeholders. You will need to establish and maintain their trust. The best way, in my experience, to achieve that trust is to be open and honest and to communicate thoughtfully, effectively and regularly with all affected stakeholders.

Communicating thoughtfully requires that you carefully consider the impact of your communication upon the recipient. Standing in front of your employees and crying out, "We are about to go under!" is not going to instil a great deal of confidence in your employees about the future of their jobs. Telling your suppliers that you have run out of cash may well trigger COD terms that will only make things worse from a cash perspective. Thoughtful communications will deliver the bad news, tempered with hope and optimism based on a strategy to overcome the problems. If you are going to secure the support of stakeholders, you will need to be able to articulate a credible turnaround strategy that will result in the restoration of your business to a healthy state, such that the stakeholder is clearly better off supporting you than dumping you. Your objective with communication is to establish in your stakeholders confidence in your plan, and trust in your ability to deliver on that plan. Regular, ongoing communications will be directed at maintaining the trust and confidence of your stakeholders in the progress of the plan and the likelihood of a successful outcome.

Rule No. 6 – Understand and acknowledge your weaknesses and vulnerabilities

A turnaround involves constantly identifying, managing, and re-solving the threats that can lead to the failure of your business. It is, therefore, essential that you understand the threats, monitor them, and have strategies in place to manage those threats and, ultimate-ly, to resolve them. This will also involve some examination (includ-ing self-examination) on the part of management to ensure that all threats, weaknesses and vulnerabilities are understood and effec-tively managed. Threat analysis is a very significant and ongoing process in any successful turnaround plan. New threats – emerging issues or unforeseen events – will emerge as old threats are overcome, and may negatively impact the success of your turnaround plan or the survival of your business.

Rule No. 7 – Be the master of your own destiny

This rule is one that I believe should be followed by every owner of a business that is in trouble. It is a principle that requires that you maintain control of the turnaround process and, at the same time, accept accountability and responsibility for the outcome of the turnaround process. No-one knows your business like you do, and no-one has more at stake than you do. So, while you may take advice from professional advisers, it is you who, at the end of the day, must make the decisions. Do not fall into the trap of abrogating responsibility to your advisers. Do not cede control of the turnaround to others. By all means, use the resources available to you to get the job done in a timely manner, but retain the ultimate decision-making authority and exercise that authority. If you do this you will be the master of your destiny. At the same time, don't be arrogant about your position. Be open to the ideas of others and give them a fair hearing. Try to consider all options and objectively assess the options available. That extends to considering your own strengths and your own shortcomings. If you assess that you are not cut out for the tough decisions that are required in a turnaround, then by all means let someone else play an active role in implementing those decisions. This does not mean you should not retain the final say. In a turnaround it is vital that you work on, rather than in, the business.

If you apply these rules to guide you in organising, developing, prioritising, and implementing your turnaround strategy, you will remain focused on the important issues, have rigorous, disciplined processes to manage and monitor your plan, and give yourself the very best chance of succeeding.

Rule No. 8 – Keep it in perspective

With so much at stake, it is easy to lose perspective when your business is in trouble. Keeping your world in balance is critical to both the success of your turnaround and to your life beyond the turnaround. There is further discussion of the importance of keeping your position in perspective in Chapter 12 under the heading of "Managing yourself".

4. Preparing for a turnaround

A word of advice: Prepare yourself

At the outset, some important words of advice. The pressures of a business in difficulty can create enormous stresses on you and those around you. Let's face it, you are dealing with the potential loss of everything you have worked hard for, and probably everything you own – so why wouldn't you be stressed? These stresses are often sustained over a long period of time and they can cause anxiety, sleeplessness, depression, and a range of other health concerns. They can cause you to become aggressive or argumentative, to lose concentration and focus, and to lose sight of your perspective and priorities.

Where these stresses are allowed to intrude into the home, it is not uncommon for business failure to lead to family breakdown and divorce. In rare cases, business failure can also lead to suicide. It is most important, therefore, that you properly manage the most important element of your turnaround strategy – you.

Difficult circumstances can cause your mind to become clouded and confused. The longer these conditions continue, the more likely it is that your thinking will be disrupted. This is perfectly normal, as the strains of managing a business in serious trouble usually result in extreme physical and psychological reactions that can disrupt clear thinking.

Without you, there is little chance that your strategy will be successfully implemented. It is unlikely that anyone else is going to take up the fight on your behalf (and even if someone did, they would not be as committed as you) so you must be 100 per cent mentally fit to succeed. Without a clear, logical, and resolute mindset, you will not be able to do your best. Turning your business around requires you to be at your very best.

Things you can and should do to keep on top of the role you will have to play in the turnaround of your business are further considered in Chapter 12. Take the time to read and follow the guidelines provided. They will help to maximise the prospects of success

What are you trying to achieve?

Every plan needs to have objectives that the plan seeks to achieve. Your goal will obviously be to get your business out of trouble. But achieving that goal will only be a temporary fix if you don't remedy the underlying causes of the problems being experienced by your business.

As explained in Chapter 1, there are a number of possible causes or factors that, alone or in combination, contribute to a business failing. By now, you should have an understanding of which of those causes apply to your business. Remedying the causes of the problems is your primary objective. This will inevitably involve a commitment of resources (time and money), a commitment to success, perseverance and a lot of personal stress.

Don't assume that things are going to get better

Every business goes through cycles and, therefore, every business suffers ups and downs. Most business managers have experienced normal trading cycles and are equipped to respond to those cycles. I have often heard business managers say, "Everybody's doing it tough – things can only get better, all we have to do is ride it out. It's only a matter of time before things go back the way they were." They might be right or they might be wrong. Two things are certain: first, there is no guarantee that things *will* return to the way they were and, second, there is no certainty as to *when* they might return to the way they were. Many serious trading declines have, initially, been seen as a normal business cycle and managers have assumed that trading will return to normal in time. Since the Global Financial Crisis (GFC) of 2007–2009, the "normal" business cycle has been disrupted, and continues to be disrupted, by macro-economic influences and government intervention. This means it is increasingly difficult to rely upon the assumption that a downturn in business is cyclical in nature and that the market will return to normal within a reasonable period of time.

One of the key points where denial is evident is in the failure to acknowledge that the circumstances being experienced may persist for years, or even get worse. Few managers consider that the current economic circumstances may last for a decade or more. Even fewer recognise that a decline in asset values may also be long-lasting.

Can the problem be fixed?

Before you commit your resources to turning around your business, it is very important to objectively consider whether or not your business can be made sustainably viable via the turnaround process. Most businesses that are experiencing problems can be turned around, but not all. In some cases, there are fundamental changes to the business environment that mean that, no matter what steps you take, you will not be able to make the business viable.

Most businesses that become unviable do so as a result of one (or more) of these three events:

1. Competition from larger and better funded competitors. No-where is this more evident than in the retail sector where the "category killer" retailer has decimated retail spaces that were previously occupied by small independent businesses. Imagine, for example, that a major "category killer" hardware store opened next to a small hardware store. It is highly unlikely that the small hardware store will ever be able to retain or capture enough sales to be sustainably profitable. Even if it could, it is more than likely that the large competitor will use its size to wage a price war that will ultimately force the smaller business out.

2. Technological change. This is a significant contributor to business failure in the current age of disruptors. It wasn't that long ago that video stores were everywhere. Now they have ceased to exist. Do you remember photo labs? Technology has made VCRs, fax machines, floppy disks and many other products obsolete. The internet is completely reshaping the way we buy goods and services, pay our bills, organise travel, and communicate with each other. Businesses that deliver these goods and services in the old way are destined to become obsolete in time.

3. Changes to government regulations which may preclude or restrict specific business activities, impose new taxes or charges, or otherwise make it difficult or impossible for a business to compete. These changes are often politically motivated and may be driven by public concerns over political issues such as trade embargos or tariffs, human rights, animal welfare, or environmental issues. They are generally unpredictable and unexpected.

As these examples illustrate, there are circumstances where, no matter how good a manager you are, the business environment will not allow your business to trade profitably on a sustainable basis. Sustainable profitability is the key to survival of any business. The situation where there is little likelihood of returning the business to sustainable profitability will, in most circumstances, be obvious. That is not to say that you should not consider all possible options to save or continue business before you give up. It does mean that the manner in which you approach the problems being experienced will be different. It may be that the business can be reinvented, re-structured or relocated, that you can adopt new technologies, or that you can find new ways to overcome potentially fatal impediments to continuing in business.

It is much more common for the prospects for the future viability of the business to be less black-and-white. A turnaround process will involve risks, strains on professional and personal relationships, and a significant investment of your time and money. Before you go down this path, it is prudent for you to consider whether the circumstances that have led to the problems being experienced by your business are such that it will not be possible to restore the business to sustainable profitability. This will not always be an easy question to answer at the outset. It will involve an assessment of the resources required to turn the business around compared to the resources available.

One business I worked with suffered a catastrophic failure of a key piece of manufacturing equipment that was imported. It would take a year to replace with no production possible in the meantime. They could replace the machine and cover costs via their insurance, but replacing the customers they were going to lose to competitors in the meantime was likely to be very hard, costly, and risky. The owners decided to exit the business rather than risk significant capital in re-growing the customer base. Another former client of mine had a contagious disease infect their herd of cattle, leading to not only the destruction of their herd but also the extended quarantining of their property. They calculated that they would need eighteen months to rebuild the herd and require $2 million in funding to get through the rebuilding. Although they were keen to start again, they didn't have that sort of money and couldn't borrow it, so they sold up and started again with a much smaller property many miles away. As another example, imagine what would happen to your business if you ran a small supermarket and a major supermarket chain opened a store right next door to your business? I recall one client in a small rural town with a small supermarket which they had run successfully for a decade, when two major supermarkets opened in town within a short space of time. These two behemoths vigorously competed for customers, making the business environment for the small supermarket almost impossible. They tried a lot of tactics to keep afloat but ultimately went broke trying to retain their business. One key message here is that it is not just a question of whether your business is capable of being turned around; it is also a question of whether or not you have the capacity to keep the business trading while the turnaround is implemented.

Technological change, as mentioned before, is another potentially fatal game changer. Think about video hire stores, manufacturers of facsimile machines or VCRs, and film processing labs. Where are they now?

From my experience, most of you will be absolutely confident that you can turn your business around and make it viable again. For those of you who are less sure of whether the business can be returned to sustainable profitability, you should keep this question in mind and under constant review as you go through the turnaround process – and be prepared to exit the turnaround process if you reach the conclusion that your efforts are futile. As the turnaround process involves a considerable commitment of time and effort (and usually lots of money) it will only be a worthwhile exercise, aside from the experience that might be gained, if it results in a successful turnaround.

If you do decide that trying to turn your business around isn't a viable exercise or if, during the course of the turnaround, you decide that your efforts are not going to succeed, you will still need to develop a plan to plot your course to exit the business with the minimum of risk and the maximum return. Strategies to exit your business are discussed in Chapters 13 and 14.

Are you the right person for the job?

The next question you need to ask is whether or not you are the right person to manage the turnaround process. This is not always a simple question to answer and you will need to consider this question as objectively as you can.

Turning a business around can involve many sacrifices, including a large time commitment, significant financial risk, reputational risk, personal stress, family stresses, swallowing your pride, and taking on legal risks. Embarking on a turnaround is a challenge that requires total commitment. In addition, it would be a rare turnaround that did not require some extremely difficult decisions to be taken, decisions that will not sit comfortably with many managers. Decisions that may include putting off longstanding staff members, changing traditional processes and practices, and stretching relationships with suppliers and customers. It is often necessary to acknowledge publicly that the business is in trouble and seek (sometimes beg) for assistance and support. The stresses of going through the workout process, where years of work and accumulated value are at risk, can place great strain on family relationships. Often, there is a need for a material change in the mindset of the owners and managers of the business.

Having said all of that, the best people to manage the turnaround of a business are those who have a vested interest in the business. That means you. The owners and managers of the business who have invested years of blood, sweat and tears, and who probably have most of their financial wealth tied up in the business, will unquestionably be the most committed to its successful turnaround. If you are able to accept that the survival of your business may mean having to make some very difficult decisions, and you are prepared to commit the time and effort to make it happen, then you are the right person for the job. If you are squeamish about those difficult conversations with longstanding staff, suppliers or customers, you can allow someone else to manage the day-to-day turnaround process – but under your ultimate direction and in accordance with your turnaround plan. You should not exclude yourself from controlling the key decisions in the turnaround process (Rule 7 – Chapter 3). Rather, if appropriate, you should recognise your shortcomings and seek support in these areas, engaging others to assist with those elements of the turnaround process where you are either extremely uncomfortable or out of your depth.

Consider engaging an adviser

This is an opportune time to introduce a key message. Turning a business around requires a skill set that is not the typical skill set of a business manager. As such, it makes good sense if you are not personally comfortable with the role of implementing a turnaround strategy, to seek the help of an experienced professional to act as your adviser. An experienced adviser will be invaluable as a source of advice and reassurance during the turnaround process. They should also be able to assist you to objectively assess your position and your strategies, including helping you decide if your business can be turned around, identifying and prioritising critical tasks, helping to define the role you should play in the turnaround, assisting with implementation of key strategies, and reviewing the progress of your turnaround plan. Having your strategies supported by appropriately skilled professional advisers will also add credibility to your requests for forbearance and/or financial support from your creditors and financiers.

It is very common, particularly with small to medium businesses, for management to resist incurring the cost of specialist advisers in a turnaround situation. This resistance is usually driven by a desire to conserve cash in circumstances where cash is tight and the business owner or manager is unclear about the value added by the adviser. In my experience a well-chosen, experienced adviser can make the difference between the success and failure of a turnaround. Within a properly and carefully managed budget, the cost of the adviser can be money well spent.

It is important to choose your advisers wisely. As with many other situations where people find themselves in trouble, there are always charlatans seeking to exploit an opportunity to make easy money from the difficulties of others. Seek out someone with relevant experience and in whom you believe you can trust. A specialist in business turnarounds is preferable. Your business/tax accountant should also be a part of your support team and may be able to assist in selecting a suitably qualified adviser. There are many good, experienced advisers in the market who specialise in business restructuring. Some are widely resourced but expensive, and more suited to larger businesses. Others specialise in servicing small to medium businesses. These smaller firms generally offer a narrower range of services but are more affordable.

If you do engage advisers, always remember that decisions are ultimately your responsibility. Take counsel from your advisers, carefully consider their suggestions and recommendations and use their experience, reputation and industry contacts to your advantage. However, it is ultimately your business, your financial position, your reputation, and your business relationships that are at risk. Your advisers are engaged to help you to maximise the prospects of a successful outcome. They are not there to make decisions on your behalf.

Additional tips to help you through a turnaround

Spend time thinking strategically

Another very important element of any successful turnaround strategy will be taking the time to think about your business. There is an old saying that managers should spend time working *on* their business rather than working *in* the business. What this saying means is that managers should not allow themselves to get distracted by the day-to-day activities involved in running a business but, rather, they should spend time thinking strategically about where the business is going and how they are going to get it to where they wish to go. This adage is even more important in a workout situation than in normal management situations.

As we will discuss later, your turnaround strategy must take the form of a plan of action. It will be up to you and your advisers to formulate, develop, and implement that plan of action. You must take the time to extract yourself from involvement in the day-to-day activities of the business so you can spend time thinking about what needs to be done to turn your business around. You will find that you will be better able to think strategically after you have cleared your headspace and if you maintain a balanced mindset and a healthy body.

Thinking strategically will invariably require discipline and perseverance as well as an open and clear mind. Spending time thinking strategically about your position should be practised every day. This will be your opportunity to drive the solutions from a strategic perspective. There will, of course, be occasions when you will need to share your thoughts and develop strategic plans in consultation with your professional advisers. This should not be substituted for personal time alone and without distraction, where you can think about the strategic issues that need to be resolved and how you will resolve them.

No doubt there will be times when you consider that you simply do not have the time to spend thinking strategically about your business, perhaps because the day-to-day pressures of the business seem to take up all of your time. A useful step is to look at the total amount of time you have available in a week and apportion that time to the priority activities that must be completed. There are 168 hours in a week. If you sleep eight hours a night and spend two hours a day getting ready for work and ready for bed, that will use up 70 hours per week. That leaves 98 hours a week for work, family, and yourself (including the time by yourself that you will need to think strategically about your business). Even if you work 50–60 hours a week in the business, you will still have 38–48 hours every week (that's five to seven hours per day) to share between your family and the things you need to do by yourself. That should be more than adequate time to find an hour every day to think strategically about your turnaround plan and what you need to do going forward.

An important part of the planning for the turnaround of your business will be planning and managing your own time. You should regularly plan your time and review how effective the use of your time has been. Time is a finite resource and during a turnaround process it is a resource that must be used as effectively as possible.

Be committed to success

If your turnaround is going to be successful, you will need to invest in the survival of your business. That means committing fully to the job of turning your business around.

Businesses experiencing troubles often have tight cash flows and, consequently, there is always a reluctance to spend money at a time when money is hard to come by. This can be a case of being "penny wise and pound foolish", as there will be times during the work-out process where it is necessary to invest in the survival of your business.

5. An overview of the turnaround process

When your business is experiencing some form of trouble, your key objective is to return it to health. Turning your business around requires a disciplined and coordinated strategy. It doesn't really matter what business you are in. Although there will be differences from business to business and industry to industry, the fundamental principles that guide the turnaround process are common to all businesses. Turning your business around will require that five fundamental steps be followed. There is a sixth step, post-turnaround, which involves ensuring the problems your business has encountered are never repeated again.

Step 1 – Acknowledge and understand the problem

When a business is in trouble the problems, left untreated, can multiply and spread. Early recognition and treatment of the symptoms can greatly enhance the prospects of a successful turnaround. One of the most common mistakes made by the owners and managers of troubled businesses is taking too long to acknowledge that there is a problem. Understanding and acknowledging your true position is the first and most important step in the process of saving your business. Many businesses fail because their owners and/or managers either don't understand there is a serious problem or they don't respond to their predicament early enough. Often, they fail to understand or refuse to accept the gravity of their situation. It is critical that you objectively assess your circumstances. In doing so you must be completely honest about where your business stands. This is not always easy, but it is essential. It is widely acknowledged by insolvency practitioners that delays in acknowledging, and responding to, the problems being experienced by a business are the major reason why many businesses ultimately fail. As explained in Chapter 2, the further down the distress staircase a business is before remedial action is attempted, the fewer the options available, and the less time available to implement a turnaround strategy.

If you fail to understand your position you will almost certainly fail to take appropriate action to remedy the situation. You must confront head-on the problems that face you and your business. In order to confront your problems, you must understand not only what those problems are but also what is causing the problems.

As part of this process, consider whether or not you are objective in your assessment of the position. You may be biased or overly optimistic. You may be too close to the business to see its flaws, vulnerabilities and weaknesses. It may be helpful to have an experienced person take an independent view of the position of your business. An independent expert may be able to help you identify if there is a problem and help you to find solutions. Never be afraid to take advice and never be afraid to admit you made mistakes. Pride can be a disastrous impediment to acknowledging and solving problems with your business.

The very fact that you are reading this book indicates that you have probably passed this first hurdle.

Step 2 – Analyse your position to identify the causes of the problem and any imminent threats

Once you have acknowledged there is a problem, you need to understand the cause (or causes) of the problem, and whether or not it can be fixed. Chapter 1 explains the causes of business failure – one or more of these causes will be applicable to your business. The causes are not always plainly visible, but there are always symptoms in evidence that can lead us to the cause or causes of the problems. Identifying the high-level causes can be a fairly simple process in some cases. However, in most cases it will be necessary to drill down into the operational aspects of the business to identify the factors that are contributing to the causes of the problems. This will require careful consideration, independent thought processes, and an impartial eye cast upon the historical trading performance of the business, its environment and current trading conditions. Ultimately, no turnaround strategy will be successful unless you identify and address the underlying cause or causes of the troubles being experienced by the business. As part of this process, it will be necessary to make some important judgement calls, including whether or not you need expert help to manage the turnaround process.

Step 3 – Stabilise the business and manage imminent threats

In a crisis situation, the short-term focus must be on keeping the business alive. A business in crisis will always demonstrate symptoms, some of which may be potentially fatal if not addressed quickly. The immediate priority must be to develop strategies to manage the immediate threats to the business. These emergency responses will need to be overlaid with a process to address the underlying causes. Often, without urgent action to remedy the symptoms, the business will fail before the underlying causes can be remedied. Although the ultimate objective of a turnaround is to fix the underlying causes of the problems in the business, the priority is to treat any immediate symptoms that represent a threat to the survival of the business first, as part of an overall strategy designed to also remedy the underlying causes. It is important that your turnaround strategy includes an ongoing assessment of the prevailing symptoms and the immediate threat they represent, and an action plan to manage those threats throughout the turnaround process.

Step 4 – Plan, organise, and implement your strategy

Having a turnaround plan will provide you with the structure necessary to undertake the turnaround process in an orderly, disciplined and timely manner. Your plan will identify your objectives, outline your turnaround strategies, and define a series of tasks to be completed to manage threats and remedy the cause/s of the problems afflicting your business.

Without a plan it is easy to become distracted by day-to-day pressures, to lose sight of what is important, to fail to properly prioritise tasks, and to miss critical timeframes. Like many circumstances in business and in life, there will be options and strategies available that will range from simple and certain to complex and highly uncertain.

Even if you decide that the problems cannot be fixed you will still need to make a plan to exit your current position with minimal financial losses and minimal reputational damage.

Step 5 – Monitor, review, and modify

Implementing your turnaround plan will require you to undertake five key roles:

1. Managing the allocation of resources to complete each of the tasks within their allotted timeframes, including managing imminent threats to the business.
2. Managing relationships with stakeholders.
3. Monitoring performance against the turnaround plan and identifying any issues or events that are impacting upon the turnaround plan or threatening the business.
4. Responding to any new threats that emerge during the turnaround process.
5. Regularly reviewing and modifying your turnaround plan to adapt to the changes in the operating environment and the business as the turnaround progresses, including assessing new opportunities that emerge to assist with the turnaround process.

Step 6 – Make sure it never happens again

The final step in the turnaround process is to implement strategies designed to ensure that the business never experiences serious troubles again.

The turnaround process on a page

ACKNOWLEDGE that there is a problem

↓

ANALYSE your position to identify the causes of the problem and any imminent threats

↓

STABILISE the business and **MANAGE** imminent threats

↓

PLAN, **ORGANISE** and **IMPLEMENT** your turnaround strategy

↓

MONITOR, REVIEW and **MODIFY** the turnaround process

↓

MAKE SURE IT NEVER HAPPENS AGAIN

6. Analysing your current position

Taking stock of your current position is the first step in developing a turnaround plan. This will involve a thorough assessment of the financial position of your business; the resources available to you to use in the turnaround process; and identifying, assessing and prioritising the threats facing your business, the risks they represent, and your ability to manage those threats.

Once you have a clear understanding of your current position, you will then have the foundation of your turnaround plan. The information you gather will help you to define your priorities, your capacity to undertake your turnaround plan, the constraints you face, and the opportunities available to you. With this information you will be able to establish realistic and deliverable goals for your turnaround plan, and develop strategies to achieve those goals that will incorporate achievable milestones and forecasts that are supported by sustainable and justifiable assumptions.

There are four outcomes you should be seeking from an analysis of your current position:

1. An understanding of the causes of the problems being experienced by your business.

2. A full understanding of the current and prospective financial position of your business. This involves an objective assessment of the cash flow and profitability of the business looking forward, as well as a thorough review of the assets and liabilities

(particularly current assets and current liabilities) to assess the capacity of the business to meet its financial obligations, its ability to withstand financial stress, and the extent of liabilities that have been incurred.

3. A complete understanding of the resources available to you to undertake and implement a turnaround. This involves identifying the resources you have that could be either used as collateral to raise debt or sold to raise cash.

4. An assessment of the threats confronting the business. This involves considering each of the key threats to the business, the level of threat they represent, and your ability to manage those threats. It will also involve understanding all of your legal rights and obligations, the legal threats that may confront you and the legal options available to you.

Your turnaround plan will not only guide your journey through the turnaround process, it will also provide you with the capacity to demonstrate to your creditors, financiers and other stakeholders that you have carefully considered the position and developed a strategy that will, on the basis of reasonable assumptions, deliver a successful turnaround.

Why is your business in trouble?

No turnaround strategy will be successful unless you identify and address the underlying cause or causes of the problems being experienced by your business. You can, and will have to, treat the symptoms, but unless the actual causes are identified and remedied, the symptoms will either persist or be only temporarily resolved, and will ultimately return. The cause of the problems may, in some cases, be very obvious – but in other cases it may be quite complicated. Identifying the underlying causes of trouble in many businesses requires careful consideration, independent thought processes, and an impartial eye cast upon the historical trading performance of the business, its environment, and current trading conditions.

In Chapter 1 we looked at the causes of business failure which, at a high level, comes down to one or more of trading losses, poor working capital management (including overtrading), lack of equity/excessive debt, and/or ineffective management. If your business is in trouble, one or more of these causes will apply. These are, however, high-level causes, and it is necessary to drill down further to locate the specific causes of the issues that your business is experiencing.

Table 2 provides an example of how to drill down on the actual causes of the problems in your business.

Table 2 – Assessing the causes of the problems in your business		
Problem	**Symptom**	**Caused by**
Trading losses or declining profits	Declining sales	• General economic downturn • A specific industry downturn • Loss of a key customer or contract • Competitor price competition • New competitor in the market • New product in the market/your products have become obsolete • Change in consumer tastes or preferences • Changes in legislation • Natural disaster/weather events
	Reducing gross profit margins	• High inflexible (fixed) production costs (factory rents, machinery costs, long-term supply contracts, labour contracts, take-or-pay contracts) • Price competition • Supplier price increases or increased government charges that cannot be passed on • Wages increasing faster than selling prices
	Excessive overheads	• Excessive administrative staff • High rents • Excess space/under-utilised space • High utility costs • Expensive service contracts
Lack of equity/poor working capital management	• Cash shortages • Overdue creditors • Tax arrears • Collection action by creditors • Defaulting on bank loans	• Funding of trading losses from trading cash flow/insufficient equity to fund losses • Cash lock-up in debtors • Cash lock-up in stock • Overtrading/growing too fast • Paying creditors too early • Debt repayments/excessive debt/rapidly rising interest rates • Excessive dividends • Seasonal trading

Understanding the financial position of your business

Financial accounts

Accurate and recent financial accounts are a genuine asset in managing a business that is in trouble. They provide a window into the business that allows the reader to understand both the profitability of the business and its financial strength, as measured by its assets and liabilities. Having consistently prepared accounts that extend over two or three trading years also facilitates the identification of trends, both favourable and unfavourable, in the performance of the business and its financial resilience. An experienced reader can quickly identify those trends and other weaknesses and vulnerabilities of the business, or areas that require more detailed analysis. Historical accounts also (generally) provide a reliable foundation for the preparation of forecasts which are essential to any turnaround plan.

If you don't have a set of recent accounts for your business, take the time to prepare one or have one prepared by your accountant. You cannot accurately assess your position without a clear understanding of the assets and liabilities of your business and the elements that are impacting upon its profitability. Make this a priority. It will be money well spent. Business owners and managers often resist preparing formal accounts and keeping them up-to-date because they are unwilling to incur the cost of having accounts prepared and do not see the benefit of incurring the cost. This attitude is folly. My experience has been that one of the key management weaknesses in businesses that fail is the lack of regular financial reporting, or a failure to review and understand the information available in financial reports. If you don't understand how to read or interpret the accounts of your business, don't be afraid to ask your accountant or adviser for assistance.

Financial forecasts

There are two key forecasts you should prepare and regularly update – a three-way monthly forecast for the next twelve months, and a weekly cash flow forecast for the next thirteen weeks (quarter-year).

A three-way forecast is a forecast which comprises three parts – the profit and loss forecast (income and expenses), balance sheet forecast (assets and liabilities), and a cash flow forecast for the business. Each of these three forecasts are inextricably linked, with changes in any one affecting each of the others. A three-way forecast allows for assumptions to be varied and the impact of those variations to be seen. This allows management to conduct sensitivity analysis to assess, for example, the impact of changes to key variables such as sales, gross profit margin, overheads, asset purchases and sales, stock levels, and capital expenditure. This type of forecast provides a full picture of the impacts of trading and non-trading activities on the financial position of the business. It also allows management to conduct scenario analysis for changes such as extending the terms of creditor payments or collecting debts more rapidly.

If you do not have a three-way forecast available, you will not be alone. Unfortunately, very few small to medium businesses prepare and use three-way forecasts as a regular business management tool, although every reasonably-sized business should have one. You should talk to your accountant about having a three-way forecast prepared.

A weekly cash flow forecast for the next thirteen weeks (three months) serves two key purposes. It provides a:

- detailed insight into the short-term cash flow needs of the business and, as such, it provides a tool for short-term cash flow planning
- mechanism by which essential cash flow management disciplines can be developed and maintained.

A business that is in trouble almost always experiences cash flow stress. Cash flow represents its key vulnerability. Disciplined cash flow management is the most important requirement of successfully managing the turnaround of a business. The importance of detailed, accurate cash flow forecasts cannot be overemphasised.

Other snapshot information

In addition to your financial accounts and forecasts there is other key data you will need, to get a snapshot of your current situation. This information will also be necessary to prepare the three-way forecasts, and includes:

- an itemised list of all of the material assets of the business (other than debtors or stock – these are listed separately below). This might include land and buildings, plant and equipment, motor vehicles, and other saleable items
- an aged creditor listing, which is a listing of the people to whom the business owes money, divided into monthly increments based on how long ago the invoice was issued. This will allow you to identify both the extent to which you are indebted to your creditors and the amount owed to creditors that is outside of normal trading terms
- current statements from the relevant tax authority showing your tax arrears (if any) and lodgements
- an aged debtor listing, which is a listing of the people who owe your business money, divided into monthly increments based on how long ago your invoice was issued. This will allow you to identify both the total amount that your business is owed and those debtors who have not paid you within normal trading terms
- a list of all debt facilities (including motor vehicle and equipment leasing and hire purchases) showing the current balance of the facility, monthly payment commitments, and the expiry

date of the facility. With respect to each monthly payment (other than leasing and hire purchase), find out if the payment is interest-only or a combination of principal and interest. You should also understand the security arrangements supporting each facility, including guarantees provided by related entities, directors, and others

- a list of all current contractual commitments (other than debt facilities) that require the business to make future payments that are formally committed. This might include forward orders with suppliers, property leases, maintenance contracts or similar commitments. If you have such arrangements that are not formally contracted, add them to the list but note them as not being formally contracted
- a recent itemised stocktake including, if possible, any information that may assist in identifying obsolete or slow-moving stock
- a list of all marketable securities (shares and bonds) held by the business
- details of all bank accounts and their current balances
- a list of all your current staff, including their role and their current remuneration.

Assessing the snapshot data

The next step in the process is to critically review all the data that you collected, to provide you with a snapshot of the business with the purpose of identifying immediate threats and opportunities.

FINANCIAL ACCOUNTS

Review your financial accounts to assess the profitability of your business (and trends in the profitability of your business), trends in sales and gross profit margin, movements in key expenses, and to identify the assets and liabilities of the business (which can be checked against the listings discussed below). If the available financial accounts cover two or more trading years, they will provide an excellent tool for trend analysis, both in terms of key profitability metrics and in terms of movements in the key assets and liabilities of the business (such as cash, stock, debtors, creditors, and debt).

Your financial accounts should also confirm the causes of the problems being experienced by your business, and allow you to drill down on individual items that might be contributing to the problems.

ASSET LISTING

Start with the itemised list of the assets of the business (other than stock and debtors). This list is likely to comprise predominantly items of plant and equipment. Review every item on the list and mark each one as "critical", "necessary", "useful" or "surplus". Critical assets will be those that are absolutely essential for the business to continue to function. Necessary assets will be those that are highly desirable but not essential (this will include assets that are not being used because there is insufficient demand at the present time, but that will be required if sales pick up). Useful assets are those assets that are used in the business but are either only used when a certain infrequent type of work arises, or are handy but not essential to the core business. Surplus assets are those that have either passed their use by date or are not currently being utilised in the business and are unlikely to be required in the short term.

You should also consider whether or not a saleable asset that may be critical or necessary can be obtained externally on a rental basis (so you may be able to sell your asset to raise cash and rent an equivalent asset back from someone else) or might be suitable for a sale and leaseback arrangement with a financier (usually such items would be fairly new and of relatively high unit value).

For those items that have been assessed as being useful, surplus, or capable of being rented or leased back, make an estimate of the value of the asset, being realistic about what it might be worth on the open market in a relatively-quick sale scenario.

CREDITORS LISTING

Assess each creditor in terms of their importance to your business, perhaps by ranking them from 1 to 5, where "1" is a critical creditor who is essential to the ongoing trading of your business and "5" is a creditor who is no longer being used, whose products or services are not likely to be required for some time, or where an alternative supplier of the same products or services on a competitive basis is readily available.

Now, review the list again, and rate each creditor from A to E, where "A" is a creditor to whom you have a firm obligation to pay within a specific timeframe (such as a legal contract), and where you consider that failure to comply with the terms of any payment obligation will result in immediate action by the creditor. It is likely that very few creditors will fit into this category. Such a creditor might include one who has issued a statutory demand that cannot be defended or a critical creditor that you anticipate will withdraw supply if not paid on time. "B" creditors will be creditors who are critical to the business, whose account is seriously overdue, and who might take action such as cutting off your account or placing you on COD in the immediate future. "C" creditors will be important creditors where you consider immediate action is unlikely, but where the relationship needs to be very carefully managed to avoid supply being cut off or a statutory demand being issued. "D" creditors will be necessary creditors whose accounts are not overdue or who are used infrequently, or who are considered to be replaceable. Creditors rated "E" will be creditors who are considered extremely unlikely to take any enforcement or recovery action (such as related parties).

During this review try to be totally impartial and avoid giving creditors a priority ranking simply because you feel a moral or personal obligation to pay them at a certain time. Commitments based on non-essential criteria can be noted separately, but should be entertained only when there is capacity for the business to make payments without threatening its survival. Also, even with critical suppliers, consider whether it might be possible to revert to COD terms and pay off the current debt. This will be determined by an assessment of the business relationship and the commercial merits of deferring payment of the current creditor liability and reversion to COD terms. All of your creditors will now be rated from "1A" (highest priority) to "5E" (least priority) and you can quantify the dollar amount that fits into each of these priority categories.

You may choose to do this analysis in a different way to better suit your needs. The important thing is that you need to understand where the threats lie in your creditor listing and where the opportunities to extend payment exist if you need to conserve cash. This analysis should be reviewed as part of your monthly review process to ensure you keep all threats from creditors under close monitoring.

You should also take a look at each of the credit application forms lodged with your suppliers and service providers to assess the level of your personal liability for the debt. Most credit application forms include personal guarantees from directors. Some also extend to creating a charge over any property owned by the director. In these circumstances it is not unusual for creditors to lodge a caveat over any real property owned by the director to secure the repayment of the debt. Where personal liability exists, the consequences of action by the relevant creditor are obviously more serious.

TAXATION AUTHORITY STATEMENTS

The taxation authority represents a significant threat to your business if you have substantial arrears and you are not taking action to reach some form of agreement about how and when you are going to repay those arrears. It is much better to be proactive and discuss your concerns with the taxation authority than to wait until they contact you or take action against your business. It is common for businesses in trouble to also become tardy about lodging tax returns with the taxation authority, usually in the hope that they can defer payment. Such a strategy is not recommended, and open and honest discussions with the taxation authority regarding payment arrangements will probably result in a better outcome than burying your head in the sand.

DEBTORS LISTING

When you review your debtors listing, look for customers who have been slow in paying you and whom you might chase for immediate payment where payment is overdue. You should also review your debtors listing and assess which of your customers really need the goods and services you provide, and those with whom you have a very strong relationship. These are customers you may be able to approach for prompt payment if you have an urgent need for cash.

DEBT FACILITIES

When you review your debt facilities you should look to get a good understanding of all of the current facilities, the payment obligations under those facilities, and the cost of those facilities. You may find opportunities by discussing your facilities with your banker and requesting that the bank review its fees and interest charges. Reductions in these charges will be extremely difficult if you are already in default of your facilities, but you may be able to request some relief from debt repayments for a while. You should also understand when all balloon payments are due and when each of your facilities expires, as these are a particular vulnerability. Strategies for extracting support from your bank are discussed in Chapter 11.

CONTRACTUAL COMMITMENTS

Review all of your contractual commitments so you have a very good understanding of what you are obliged to do and pay under each of these formal arrangements. Look at the maturity date of each arrangement and consider whether there is an opportunity to either terminate the arrangement or reduce the cost of the arrangement going forward.

STOCKTAKE

Review your stocktake critically to determine if you are carrying excess, obsolete or slow-moving stock. These can all be a useful source of quick cash.

MARKETABLE SECURITIES AND CASH AT BANK

Marketable securities and cash at bank represent the most readily accessible sources of cash for your business. These assets provide immediate capacity to meet urgent financial commitments.

STAFF LISTING

One of the most difficult tasks that the manager of a troubled business faces is the prospect of having to retrench staff to reduce the costs of the business. You should review your staff listing, consider what each person contributes to the business operation, and identify those people who are essential to the business. This is not necessarily an easy analysis and often requires a lot of thought, as most managers consider that all of their staff are essential to the business for one reason or another. At this stage of the planning process, all you are seeking to do is to identify potential opportunities to reduce costs if necessary.

Assessing the resources available to you

The resources identified by your analysis represent your starting position, what you have available to you now, and what you owe to others. It will be useful to ensure that your three-way forecasts are consistent at their starting point with your assessment of the resources currently available to you and the liabilities of your business.

The review of your snapshot data should make it relatively easy to identify the resources that are available to you to aid in your turn-around strategy. These resources will consist of:

- cash and assets that can be readily turned into cash, such as marketable securities
- physical assets that will be necessary to continue the business. Such assets will include essential trading stock, production inputs, premises, delivery vehicles, production machinery, and anything else that is essential to continued trading. In preparing this list you should also identify those assets within the list that might be suitable for sale and leaseback arrangements if the need arises, such as land and buildings, and larger, relatively new items of plant and equipment
- assets that are not essential to continued trading that may be saleable as a means to raise cash. These assets are not limited to plant and equipment but might also include excess or obsolete trading stock, production inputs that are not essential for continued trading, and investment real estate. The list of assets may include personal assets that are surplus to immediate requirements that might be sold to inject funds into the business if necessary
- employees who you consider to be essential to the ongoing success of the business
- people with whom you have a very strong and longstanding relationship and to whom you might turn if a critical need for

support arises. This list may include customers, suppliers, business contacts, family and friends.

Having a list of the resources available to you will assist you in the planning of your turnaround strategy.

Understand your legal position

Providing legal advice is beyond the scope of this book. It is strongly recommended that you seek independent legal advice as soon as you become aware that your business is experiencing trading difficulties, to ensure you understand the legal framework within which your turnaround will be operating.

Every business operates within a statutory framework that defines the rights and obligations of the business, its customers, its suppliers, its financiers and its shareholders. In every jurisdiction there are legal obligations imposed upon businesses that are designed to avoid businesses taking on credit and financial obligations that they cannot repay. In most instances, these obligations impose potentially serious penalties upon the directors of businesses who intentionally or negligently trade their business while it is insolvent. In some instances, directors and managers of businesses may become personally liable for debts incurred where a business continues to trade while insolvent.

There are also laws in every jurisdiction that provide rights for creditors to take action against businesses that have not paid them in accordance with the agreed terms. These laws generally allow a dissatisfied creditor to serve demands upon the business for the monies owing and to seek the appointment of an administrator to the business if the debt is not subsequently paid.

A number of jurisdictions also provide legal avenues for temporary protection or shelter for businesses that are experiencing problems.

For example, in the USA there is provision for what is known as Chapter 11 protection in certain circumstances. In the UK, Australia, and New Zealand, there are voluntary administration arrangements available in some circumstances to provide temporary protection from action by creditors. Similar arrangements exist in many other jurisdictions.

Businesses also incur contractual obligations where the rights and obligations of the parties to the agreement are set out in the form of written contractual agreements that are binding on the parties. Most businesses will have contractual obligations in the form of property tenancy agreements and financing contracts. Many businesses will also have contractual relationships with their suppliers (in particular, agreements specifying credit terms), customers and staff. The nature and extent of contractual obligations will vary dramatically from business to business. These obligations should be identified and reviewed as part of the process of preparing for your turnaround so that you have a good understanding of what your contractual obligations are, and what the potential impacts are if you breach your contractual obligations. If it becomes apparent in the course of the planning or implementation of your turnaround that you will breach your contractual obligations, you should seek early legal advice to assess the alternatives available to manage the risks that may arise as a result.

7. Stabilising your business

There is no point trying to turn your business around if the business fails while you are developing and implementing your turnaround strategies. In a crisis situation your priority focus must be on keeping the business afloat. In many cases, immediate actions will be necessary to neutralise or stabilise imminent threats to prevent the business failing, and so your first and most important objective is to identify and implement strategies to manage these immediate threats. These will be emergency responses with short-term target outcomes that will then need to be overlaid with a process to address the underlying causes.

A business experiencing serious problems will face a number of threats to its survival. As the business moves further down the distress staircase (Chapter 2, p 44), the frequency and urgency of the threats will increase. In the vast majority of cases those threats will be a result of a shortage of cash. Action by creditors, revenue authorities or financiers are the most common threats in this space that can lead to potentially fatal outcomes. In some cases, threats will not be cash related. These circumstances might include the impacts of loss of critical personnel, partnership disputes, a major computer meltdown, litigation, natural disasters, changes to laws, and loss of approvals or licences necessary to operate the business.

It will be crucial, as part of your turnaround process, to take steps to identify, overcome, mitigate, and/or manage imminent threats to your business. It will also be necessary to maintain a continuing process to monitor and manage threats throughout the turnaround process, as new threats will constantly emerge and existing threats that are only being managed (rather than overcome) will remain in the background and may re-emerge quickly. An important part of any turnaround strategy will include a regular (if not constant) reassessment of the imminent threats and risks facing the business, and ongoing management of those threats throughout the turnaround process.

Identifying and assessing threats to your business

Threats to your business are events that can adversely affect your income, increase your expenses, reduce your profit margins or endanger the very survival of your business. Identifying threats to a business that is in trouble is quite different to identifying threats to a business that is trading normally. The threats to a troubled business will be more specifically identifiable, more imminent, and generally more measurable. A business in trouble will also experience a higher number of potentially fatal threats.

Every business operates in a dynamic environment and faces a variety of factors that may damage the business or, in extreme circumstances, cause it to fail. These threats have three basic sources:

- external – threats that arise from sources outside of the business
- internal – threats that exist or arise from inside the business
- personal – threats that originate from the personal circumstances of the owners or senior executives of the business.

External threats

External threats are the most common threats to business, and include such events as economic downturns, competition from competitors, substitute products, social change, new technology, and government regulation. External threats are usually difficult to predict, come with little notice, and can often have very serious consequences for a business.

In the case of a business experiencing problems, external threats are much more likely to include debt collection action by unpaid creditors, enforcement action by taxation authorities, and/or debt recovery action by your bank. Most external threats to a business are serious and many are potentially fatal. They are characterised by the need to manage or mitigate the acts or actions of external parties which is often very difficult.

Internal threats

There are many internal threats within any business and a number of these arise or are accentuated when a business is having problems. They are broadly related to three elements of the business:

- People – A business experiencing difficulties creates uncertainty for staff. Most people live from pay packet to pay packet, and depend on that next pay to get them through. Staff are also often placed under additional stress as they try to cope with the pressures of tight cash flow, complaints and resource shortages. Faced with these additional stresses and the threat of losing their jobs, staff will often look for alternative employment rather than wait to be unemployed, and this can leave the business without key people.
- Machinery – In troubled businesses it is common to see important machinery fail because it has not been properly maintained or replaced due to lack of funds.
- Systems and other threats – This includes IT failure (possibly due to loss of key staff or lack of maintenance), stock-outs (usually due to lack of funds to restock), and compliance breaches (often due to other priorities taking precedence or a lack of staff to perform compliance obligations).

Internal threats can, at least to some extent, be managed and controlled, although they are often not predicted, particularly where people are concerned. Individually, internal threats are rarely fatal, but they can be a cause of disruption and, left untreated, they can have serious and potentially fatal consequences. Stock-outs are a very good example of how an unmanaged internal threat can develop to have fatal consequences for a business. Initially, one or two stock lines are impacted by an unpaid supplier refusing to continue to supply the business, which causes sales to decline. The decline in sales results in cash shortages, which further restrict the capacity of the business to purchase stock, and so further stock-outs occur and sales decline again. As stock shortages grow, customers leave the business causing further declines in sales, and a vicious downward spiral continues until the business collapses.

Personal threats

Personal issues affecting the business owners and managers include some of the deadly D's, in particular, distraction (as a result of family conflicts and stress), divorce (a fairly common outcome, especially when the problems last for an extended period), disease (including mental health), and death (either from illness caused by constant stress or suicide).

Personal threats are a much greater threat in small to medium private businesses, where there are only one or two key managers, than they are to larger businesses. They are not often evident as a threat to businesses until they come into being. However, their impacts can be devastating to a small or medium business.

If you are going to manage the turnaround of your business, you become the key person. Any adverse change to your health, mental state, and even your level of motivation, can materially threaten both the success of your turnaround plan and the long-term future of your business.

You will probably already have a good idea of the key threats to your business, particularly those that have already crystallised, or are close to crystallising, and are having an impact upon your business. Nevertheless, take the time to stop and consider all of the other threats that may arise and threaten your business in the short term (the next few weeks or months). But, your thinking should go beyond this term to at least list those items that represent potential threats in the next six to twelve months, so that you can be prepared should those threats materialise.

Prioritising and managing the threats to your business

A business in trouble always has limited resources to combat the symptoms and causes of problems. One of the most important tasks facing the manager of such a business is to prioritise the allocation of those limited resources to the control, management or mitigation of threats. This will involve assessing threats on three levels:

1. The extent to which the threat will, if crystallised, impact upon your business.
2. Your ability to manage the threat or its impacts.
3. The immediacy of the threat.

The threats to a business experiencing difficulties will be more imminent and more serious than would ordinarily be the case (for a business that is not experiencing difficulties), with some threats having potentially fatal consequences. There will be little opportunity for you to worry about unpredictable or as-yet-unknown threats. Predictable or crystallised threats will preoccupy your time.

The significance of a specific threat is assessed by a combination of the likelihood that the event will occur, the immediacy of its occurrence, and the level of impact the event will have on your business.

- At the lowest level a threat may cause **inconvenience**.
- A more important threat might cause **moderate disruption**.
- A significant threat can cause **serious damage** to your business.
- A catastrophic threat can have **fatal consequences** for your business.

Clearly your priority should be upon those threats that could have fatal consequences for your business. But, in assessing the potential consequences of a threat, be mindful that threats that may result in inconvenience or moderate disruption in the early stages of decline may escalate to become serious, and possibly fatal, threats to the business over time.

Managing threats

The key point of difference between the threats that you will encounter when your business is in trouble is the level to which you are able to control, manage, and/or mitigate the threat.

There are only three ways to manage threats:

1. Avoid them.
2. Manage them.
3. Mitigate them (reduce or eliminate their impacts).

The best solution to managing a threat is to avoid it altogether. Avoiding business threats involves seeking to create conditions in which the threat cannot materialise or affect your business. For example, avoiding the risk of action by the taxation authority might mean ensuring that you lodge all returns on time and pay all taxes on time. In determining the most appropriate management strategy for a specific threat, you will be much more inclined to seek to avoid a threat if it has potentially fatal consequences than you will be to avoid the threat that has less significant consequences. That is going to be particularly true where the events giving rise to the fatal consequences might occur without warning. Where threats cannot be avoided, it will be necessary to consider whether they can be managed or mitigated.

Managing threats involves reducing to the extent possible (but not necessarily eliminating) the risk that the threat will materialise. You can, for example, manage the risk of a creditor taking action to collect their outstanding debt by making regular payments and keeping a good line of communication open with the creditor. This will not eliminate the threat that the creditor will take action if you are outside of their trading terms, but it will significantly reduce the risk that that particular creditor will take action against you.

Mitigating a threat involves taking action to minimise or eliminate the impact of events upon your business. Strategies to mitigate the impacts of a threat are applied where a threat has already materialised. There will be many instances where, due to a lack of resources (such as cash), it will not be possible to avoid a risk that might, in other circumstances, be avoidable. This is a common situation for a business experiencing difficulties. There are a wide variety of mitigation strategies available. In the main, mitigation strategies will involve negotiated outcomes with third parties and the careful allocation of scarce resources, often for the purpose of buying time, while a turnaround strategy is implemented. Even where a specific threat can (apparently) be managed it will be wise, where possible, to also have a mitigation plan for that threat.

The Threat Matrix

In a troubled business, avoiding, managing, and mitigating threats involves the commitment of scarce and finite resources, so it is necessary to prioritise the allocation of resources to responding to the threats to your business. This involves assessing threats in terms of the likelihood of their occurrence, and ranking threats in terms of their likely impact on the business. The assessment will result in a "threat matrix", with each significant threat ranked based on the level of damage it could cause to the business and the likelihood of occurrence. The potential damage a threat might cause can range from inconvenience to catastrophic/fatal consequences. The likelihood of occurrence will range from unlikely to certain (immediate).

There are many distractions for managers that can divert attention from a comprehensive analysis of their position. In these circumstances, threats can be overlooked or missed until it is too late. The threat matrix provides a considered and complete list of the known threats to your business and your proposed response to each. As such, it provides an immediate plan of action when an identified threat materialises. It is also a systematic way of:

- identifying the threats to your business
- assessing the potential for those threats to damage your business
- assessing your capacity to control the threats
- prioritising your responses
- allocating your limited resources
- developing strategies to remove, manage or mitigate those threats.

You will probably already have a fair idea of the immediate threats to your business and the major potential threats that might materialise in the short term. There will be others that you haven't thought about or that may not yet have manifested themselves as immediate threats to your business. Preparing the threat matrix provides you with the opportunity to both identify prospective threats that you haven't yet identified and to carefully consider your response to existing threats.

To prepare the threat matrix for your business, make a list of all the threats you are aware of and then assess each threat based on three characteristics of the threat, each of which has four levels of measurement:

1. **The likelihood of occurrence** – that is, the chances of the threat impacting your business in the near future, assessed as:

   - unlikely/improbable (not expected to be a threat in the near future)
   - possible (may arise as a threat in the near term, but no certainty about this eventuality)
   - highly likely (very likely/almost certain to become a threat in the near term)
   - certain (actions or events that will impact on the business have commenced).

2. **The expected impacts** the threat will have on your business, which will be:

   - of limited or no effect
   - moderate (impacts that will hurt the business but which can be managed without representing a threat of failure or collapse)
   - severe (the impacts will seriously impact on the business and, if not managed or mitigated, could be fatal to the business)
   - catastrophic or fatal (the impacts will almost certainly result in the appointment of an administrator or liquidator by other parties or will otherwise be fatal to the business).

3. **Your ability/capacity to control or mitigate the threat** which will be:

   - avoidable (you are able, or have already taken action, to avoid or stop the threat from impacting on your business in the near term)
   - manageable (you need to take action to minimise the impact of the threat and you believe that, while the threat may have some impact, the impact will not be serious if you take that action)

- mitigation (you cannot avoid the threat impacting on your business and the threat represents a serious or fatal threat – the only action you can take is to seek to mitigate the impacts)
- none (you cannot do anything to avoid, manage or mitigate the threat). Very few, if any, threats will fall into the "none" category, unless an administrator has already been appointed or there is enforcement action underway that will inevitably result in an administrator being appointed to the business. Note that if you cannot avoid, manage or mitigate a fatal or potentially fatal threat to the business, it is likely the business will fail, so if "none" is the control level applied to such a threat in your analysis, you may need to urgently turn your mind to deciding how you can change the control level or (if you can't) whether to continue with your turnaround strategy.

Imminent (certain) threats which have the potential to cause catastrophic or fatal damage to your business will obviously require immediate attention. There will be a range of threats which fall into less significant categories but which must also be managed to avoid the risk that they will become fatal threats to your business in the future.

Following is a simple example of a threat matrix prepared for a small manufacturing business, Manufacture Co, which is now experiencing problems as a result of its major customer, Customer Co, going into voluntary administration. This has meant that the sales made in the last three months to Customer Co (several million dollars) will not be paid, leaving Manufacture Co with a serious cash shortage and unable to pay its creditors or the taxation authority. The taxation authority is now threatening wind-up action and one supplier, Jones & Co, has delivered a statutory demand for payment which must be responded to within 21 days. Several other key suppliers are chasing their outstanding invoices and two have put Manufacture Co on COD terms. Management are unsure if they can pay the next week's wages. Staff are concerned by rumours that the business is in trouble.

Table 3 – Threat Matrix example				
Threat	Likelihood of occurrence	Potential impact	Ability to control threat	Strategy comments
Winding-up action – taxation authority	Certain	Catastrophic/ fatal	Mitigate	Seek a payment arrangement. Need to establish our capacity to repay over time so we can meet agreed repayments. Note that this is a bank default.
Creditor statutory demand – Jones & Co	Certain	Catastrophic	Mitigate	Talk to Jones – seek deferral or a staged payment plan. Note that this is a bank default.
Bank default	Certain	Severe (if not managed)	Mitigate	Triggered by taxation authority and creditor action. Will not be able to make all loan payments on time. Talk to the bank about our strategy to remove taxation authority threat and about deferring loan payments.
Continuing cash shortages	Certain	Severe to catastrophic	Manage	Talk to accountants about cash strategy. Look at sale of surplus assets and other actions to raise cash until we get through.

Table 3 – Threat Matrix example				
Threat	Likelihood of occurrence	Potential impact	Ability to control threat	Strategy comments
Unable to pay wages	Highly likely	Severe	Manage	Prepare a forward cash flow to see when this might occur. Talk to the bank about additional funding that is needed to cover wages shortfall.
Collection action or stop supply by other creditors	Highly likely	Severe to catastrophic	Manage	Talk to key suppliers. Seek terms for current debt. If necessary, COD for future deliveries while we pay off the old debt.
Competitor actions – price war	Expected	Moderate	None	Competitor Spiteful Co may seek to take advantage of our weak position. We have no capacity to respond at present but Spiteful Co is too small to take much business in the short-term.
Trading losses continuing	Unknown	Unknown	Unknown	Discuss future profitability with accountants to assess if the business can return to profitability without Customer Co's business before all our assets are exhausted.

Note that the action by the taxation authority and Jones & Co are underway, so they are "certain" events. These events are also defaults under the terms of the company's bank loan agreements, so bank default is a consequent certain event that also needs to be mitigated. The management has further recognised that without the business of Customer Co the business may not be able to trade profitably. This has been added as a threat but listed as "unknown" in all three assessment categories until further information is gathered.

Useful additions to this table would be columns for "timing" (to indicate when action will be taken or by when the threat will be managed), and "who" (to identify who is responsible for implementing the action). I recall one situation where an important payment to the taxation authority was missed because the client and his accountant both thought the other was monitoring taxation payments. This failure resulted in the taxation authority taking winding up action.

It is important to recognise that the threat matrix is not a static document but must be regularly reviewed and updated (at least monthly). Use the threat matrix as a tool to effectively manage threats.

Time is an overlooked threat

Time is not often recognised as a threat to your business, but in a turnaround situation time is a significant risk factor. Time provides the opportunity for prevailing conditions and circumstances to change and, as such, time presents uncertainty and risk. The longer it takes to achieve an objective or milestone event in your turnaround strategy, the greater the risk that it will not be achieved as a result of an unforeseen change in the business environment. That change might be a downturn in the economy, higher interest rates, weaker market conditions, increased competition, a key staff member leaving or a raft of other possible external or internal events.

Your creditors and bankers are more likely to be concerned by, and therefore less likely to support, a plan that has lengthy timeframes to achieving critical milestones. They are also more likely to take action against you if you fail to meet target timeframes.

Your plan will have to include milestone events with target timeframes. Managing the timelines in your plan will be a significant risk management issue.

Managing creditors

Almost invariably, creditors are the most serious, imminent threats to a business in a crisis situation. The creditors of your business can be broadly divided into six categories:

- **Trade creditors** are the businesses that provide credit to your business for its normal trading activities. These creditors will predominantly comprise suppliers but may also include freight companies.
- **Revenue authorities** are government departments that collect taxes in one form or another.
- **Services creditors** are those businesses that provide utilities, insurance and professional advice.
- **Landlords** are a separate group of creditors from a management perspective because they require individual strategies to manage.
- **Banks and financiers** also require different management strategies than other classes of creditors.
- **Staff** are the final distinct group of creditors that require careful management.

While there are specific strategies applicable to each individual creditor group, which will be discussed later in this chapter, there are five general principles that should be applied in the management of all creditors. These principles are simple, practical and essential to a successful turnaround.

1. Understand the legal options creditors might pursue

You should make sure that you have a good understanding of each creditor's legal options to pursue the collection of their debts. This understanding can be gained by discussing the actions available to creditors with your lawyer or accountant so you are fully aware of what action they might take and the applicable timeframes. You should also have your lawyer review credit applications, leases, and contracts with suppliers. These days, most credit applications made by small to medium businesses with suppliers include personal guarantees from directors. Credit applications from larger businesses often include a lien on the assets of the directors who have guaranteed the credit facility. It is not uncommon for creditors to pursue directors personally when a business fails. In these circumstances, creditors may attach liens or caveats to the personal property of directors to secure their rights.

The terms of supply agreements generally also include provisions that mean title to the goods supplied to your business do not pass to you until you have paid for those goods.

2. Constantly monitor your creditors

The creditors schedule you prepared as part of assessing your current position should be kept constantly updated. Review that schedule so that you clearly understand:

- who your creditors are
- how much each of them is owed
- how long their debts have been outstanding
- how significant they are to your business.

You will need to consider each individual creditor, prioritise them in terms of the threat they pose to your business, and then develop a plan to manage the relationship through the period of difficulty.

3. Communicate often and effectively

The most important principle for managing creditors is to maintain regular and effective communication with them. Time and time again I have seen businesses fail because managers have failed to effectively communicate with their key creditors. If you do nothing else to turn your business around, you must communicate effectively.

It is very common for business owners and managers to avoid communication with their creditors. In some cases, managers convince themselves that it would be a mistake to disclose their difficulties to creditors. Some fear that creditors will withdraw supply or put them on COD. Some fear that creditors will damage their reputation by spreading the word that their business is in trouble. But it is more often a function of pride, a reluctance to acknowledge the difficulties being experienced by the business. It can be embarrassing to acknowledge that you are unable to meet your financial commitments.

The problem with failing to communicate with your creditors is that it is very, very difficult to keep a business with serious problems hidden from view. Eventually, when the position becomes publicly known, any damage to the reputation of the business or to the confidence of suppliers will be magnified by a lack of trust arising from poor communication.

Effective communication instils trust and confidence. Conversely, lack of communication creates uncertainty and distrust. There is always an element of risk in communicating your circumstances to creditors. I have seen situations where creditors have taken aggressive action to protect their interests to the detriment of the honest businessperson. However, I have much more frequently seen creditors take aggressive action when they have been misled by efforts to conceal the problems.

4. Have a message

It is futile to communicate with your creditors unless you have some meaningful message to communicate to them. You will need to convince your creditors that they should continue to support your business. In order to do that, they will need to believe that your business can survive and prosper into the future, and that they will be more likely to recover the money that you owe if they support you.

You must consider the message you will communicate to your creditors. You should be able to demonstrate to your creditors that you know how to turn the business around, that you are committed to the turnaround plan, and that the turnaround plan has a reasonable prospect of success if you are supported by your creditors.

It will not be sufficient to simply talk up the future. The point here is that the message you give to your creditors must be credible and deliverable.

5. Deliver on your message

Every creditor to whom you deliver your message will expect you to make good on your undertakings and to achieve their expectations, particularly in terms of any payment promises made. Although circumstances will almost certainly change during the course of your business turnaround, you must make every effort to achieve the outcomes that you have led your creditors to expect.

In circumstances where you are unable to deliver on those promises, you must communicate the reasons and the amended outcomes to your creditors in an open and honest manner at the earliest opportunity. While it is likely that the failure to deliver on creditors' expectations will result in a loss of confidence in your ability to deliver on your plan, in most cases people will understand that plans never work out perfectly and you may still be able to secure their support if you keep open lines of communication in place.

Managing specific creditor groups

Trade creditors

Trust in business relationships is established over time. It stands to reason, therefore, that the longer the relationship between the creditor and the business, the more likely it is that the creditor will provide support or forbearance. Most business managers will have a good sense of those creditors with whom they have a trusting relationship. Noting that all business relationships are symbiotic, it is often advantageous for the creditor to support the troubled business for the longer-term benefit of their own business. In some instances, this relationship can be a critical relationship to the creditor, with their own survival threatened if the struggling business fails.

Larger businesses will generally have greater capacity to be flexible; but that will not often convert to a willingness to support customers that are in trouble. These businesses generally have a wide customer base and are less likely to suffer any material impacts if they lose the custom of a particular business. They will also have policies and procedures that will dictate their actions. These days it is also increasingly common for larger businesses to require personal guarantees from their customers' directors, so they enjoy a higher degree of leverage over the business proprietor in terms of getting priority payment.

Taxation authorities

Taxation authorities are government departments that are charged with collecting taxes. These departments usually have policies that provide for time payment arrangements (with or without interest charges) where a taxpayer is unable to meet their commitments. They will generally support taxpayers with a good history, or those who have been impacted by unforeseen natural disasters, by agreeing to deferred payment terms or a periodic repayment arrangement.

It is preferable to ask for extended payment terms early rather than waiting for the authority to chase you up before asking for some relief. A request for a payment arrangement is probably best made through your usual tax accountant.

If you have recurrent reporting obligations during the period of deferred payments, then make sure you comply with your reporting obligations in a timely manner. If you have additional or recurrent payments due during the period of forbearance, then factor these payments into your cash flows when making your request to ensure that you can meet your deferred payment plan and all of your other tax commitments. Taxation authorities are rarely disposed to providing relief when previous commitments have been breached.

Critical services creditors

Services creditors comprise those businesses that supply your business with utilities (electricity, gas, water), and communications (telephone/internet). The loss of electricity, gas, water or communications can have catastrophic consequences for your business, so it is critical that you maintain these services.

It is likely that businesses that supply utilities and communications will be large businesses that have a social agenda and will be willing to provide some degree of flexibility in their payment terms.

Many will have policies designed to support customers experiencing short-term difficulties that will allow them to provide favourable payment terms. If you are unable to pay your debts to a critical service provider you need to be proactive in making contact with your service provider, and making arrangements for deferred payment terms so you can ensure continuity of supply.

Landlords

Landlords are usually among the first to suffer non-payment when a business has cash flow issues. When non-payment of rent occurs, landlords are faced with a set of difficult circumstances. They are subject to the terms of your lease which will contain notice obligations and processes that have to be followed with respect to termination of your lease. In some jurisdictions, landlord and tenant relationships are regulated by laws that impose conditions on recovering possession of leased premises. Commercially, loss of your tenancy will impact their income, potentially for an extended period of time while they clear you out and replace you with another tenant.

As such, landlords probably have more incentive than most creditors to support your business if you have a good track record as a tenant. Most landlords will act reasonably if you can demonstrate that the situation in which you find yourself is temporary. It will assist if you have a clear strategy and timetable to restore your position to one where you have paid your rent arrears and can pay your rent on time. On the other hand, some landlords will be hard because they hold a bond or guarantee for several months' rent and they believe they can get another, better tenant within that time. There are also a few landlords who will not grant any time to pay because they consider that granting forbearance is a sign of weakness that will result in all tenants exploiting them. Hopefully you will have gleaned whether your landlord is going to be supportive or aggressive from your past dealings. Either way, you should seek advice from your lawyer so you understand exactly what the terms of your lease require of both you and the landlord when rent is in arrears, and whether there are any regulations that may impact upon the landlord's rights. These rights, obligations and timeframes can be incorporated into your risk management matrix.

Your bank and other financiers

Loan repayments are often delayed or missed when a business is experiencing cash stress. If your business is carrying debt (including financed plant and equipment) you need to be very careful about how you manage your relationship with your financiers, who usually have fairly draconian powers if you default on the terms of your loans. Chapter 11 is dedicated to helping you understand what your bank might do and how you can manage your relationship with your lenders.

Employees

Staff are another important and unique group of creditors. They are a group that require careful and effective management when your business is in trouble. Chapter 12 discusses strategies for managing your relationship with staff during difficult times.

8. Turnaround strategies

The objective of your turnaround plan is to develop and implement strategies that will resolve the problems being experienced by your business and restore it to a position of sustainable profitability and financial soundness. Keep this objective as your measuring stick for strategies as you progress through identifying and implementing the available strategy options.

Like many situations in business and in life, there will be options and strategies available that will range from simple and certain to complex and highly uncertain. In developing your strategy, you should seek to remove uncertainty and complexity wherever possible. Try to build your plan around those strategy options where you have the capacity to exercise greatest control and where you understand what has to be done and how it should be done. Try to avoid critical strategy options that depend on the actions of others or those that are complex or uncertain. As an example of what I mean, many businesses experience problems because they are undercapitalised, meaning that they have insufficient equity (owners' funds) in the business. A common strategy to turn an undercapitalised business around is to raise equity by inviting external investors to invest in the business. Although this can be an appropriate solution in some cases, raising external equity is a difficult, time consuming, expensive, and often complex process that is beyond the experience of most business managers. The message here is that, when you are reviewing any strategy option, consider carefully the complexity, timing, cost – and your ability to deliver the desired outcome.

Your turnaround strategies will incorporate one or more of the following six objectives:

1. buying time
2. improving the trading performance (sustainable profitability) of the business
3. recapitalising the business (raising equity)
4. refinancing the business
5. selling part of the business as a going concern
6. selling assets of the business.

If the circumstances of your business are dire, you may decide that threats to the business are so serious that you either do not have enough time to implement a turnaround plan, or the prospects of a successful turnaround are remote without a radical reduction of the liabilities of the business. There are still options available if the underlying business is sound and potentially profitable. These options are discussed in Chapter 14

Strategies designed to buy time

Almost every business in trouble will adopt strategies designed to buy time. These strategies are very common in turnaround plans and, in many instances, are an essential component of a turnaround plan.

Strategies to buy time will include funding strategies to keep cash flowing while the business is restored to health, sold off or recapitalised. Such strategies may include actions designed to bring forward debtor receipts, stretch creditor payments, sell off excess stock, sell off surplus plant and equipment, and/or raise additional debt funding. These options are considered in further detail in Chapter 10. Other strategies to buy time might include seeking to suspend or defer loan repayments. Chapter 11 discusses options for dealing with your bank as part of your turnaround strategy.

Strategies designed to improve trading performance

The core problem for the majority of businesses that are in trouble is trading losses. For these businesses, strategies designed to improve the trading performance of the business will be critical to the long-term survival of the business. If your business *isn't* profitable, then making your business profitable must be one of your core objectives. As discussed previously, an unprofitable business is ultimately doomed and any turnaround plan that doesn't address the absence of profitability in a business will also ultimately fail.

There are only three ways to improve the trading performance of a business:

- Increasing revenues (sales).
- Improving profit margins.
- Reducing costs.

Increasing sales

Revenue growth can be achieved by increasing sales volumes and/or increasing prices. However, in a competitive environment it is often difficult to increase sales volumes or increase prices. A very common mistake made by business managers is to set unrealistic and unachievable sales growth targets, and to rely on the resultant forecast improvement in profitability as the key to the turnaround plan. Make sure that you do not make this mistake. Be realistic about the sales growth you can achieve. If your forecasted sales growth is materially above what you achieved in the preceding year then you should consider carefully if you are being realistic or optimistic.

Be aware that your financiers and other stakeholders will ask you to justify how you will achieve significant sales growth.

Improving profit margins

It can be equally difficult to increase profit margins on sales in a competitive environment. In some cases, there may be some easy wins available when it comes to improving profit margins, such as better management of stock levels, just-in-time purchasing, sharper buying practices, and implementing mechanisation and/or technological improvements to production processes. Again, be realistic in your assessment of what you can achieve. It is very easy to make the numbers work by ratcheting profit margins up by a few percentage points, but even small gains are often difficult to achieve.

Reducing costs

Reducing costs, particularly overhead costs, is an area where there is often scope for material improvement. There are a range of areas where costs might be cut. You will need to examine your costs on a line-by-line basis and consider whether the cost is a necessary expense of the business or an optional expenditure, how you might reduce each cost, and the impact of reducing the cost on the business. Reducing some costs can result in short-term increases in costs. For example, putting off staff will often involve paying redundancy costs and paying out their accrued entitlements, which will cause an additional short-term cash burden. Reducing some costs can also result in higher costs elsewhere in the business. For example, moving your premises further out of the city may reduce your rent but increase transport costs.

Reducing staff numbers is one of the most difficult decisions that a manager ever has to make. It is always hard to deprive an employee of their employment and income. The longer the employee has been with the business, the harder it will be to let them go. There is also the loss of the employee's skills and experience to consider. The best approach is to be up-front and honest with the employee as to the reasons why the decision has been taken. It may well be that the alternative is a higher risk that the business will fail – in which case, the job will go anyway (and others with it). You might consider bringing your employees along on the turnaround journey. Employees have a vested interest in the business surviving so they will be motivated to help. There have been cases where employees have collectively agreed to accept a pay cut while the business gets back on its feet so as to keep everyone employed. On the downside, there is a risk that valuable employees will exit the business if they become concerned for their job security, but this will probably happen anyway. It is hard to keep financial stress a secret.

It is important to note that, unlike the other strategy options discussed below, improving the trading performance of your business does not automatically improve cash flow. Indeed, some measures to improve trading performance (such as increasing sales) can be a short-term drain on cash flow. It may be necessary, therefore, to pursue one or more of the following strategies in parallel with strategies designed to improve the trading performance of your business.

Recapitalising your business

Recapitalising your business involves raising equity funds from investors to bring additional cash into the business. Unlike debt equity, investors take a share of the business in return for their investment in the business. The advantage of equity is that it does not require regular payment of interest and does not have to be repaid. Equity funding does not require security as a bank loan might.

However, raising equity capital (recapitalisation) can be a lengthy and complex process. It can be a particularly difficult, frustrating, and often unsuccessful, process for a business that is in trouble.

Moreover, new equity will generally come at a high price due to the inherent risks being taken by the investor or investors. The exception will be where the equity is raised from friends and family who are often willing to invest without seeking an appropriate risk return.

Raising equity will also require having full details of the business available for prospective investors, which will usually mean the production of a detailed investment memorandum and forecasts for the business. Historical accounting records will also be a very important source of information for prospective investors. It is usually best to use an adviser with experience in equity raisings to assist with the production of investment information and the process of seeking out, and dealing with, prospective investors.

Seeking fresh equity for your business is a strategy that should be complemented with other strategy options, both to buy the time necessary for an equity-funding strategy to be implemented, and to provide an alternative if an equity-funding strategy fails. It will take time to raise equity, and many businesses have collapsed while they chased equity investors due to extensive time delays, the complexity of the equity-funding process, and the lack of understanding of these complexities on the part of management.

Refinancing your business

Refinancing your business involves securing debt funding to finance the needs of your business. Debt funding attracts regular interest charges, is usually secured against the assets of the business or the assets of the directors, and is repayable either in instalments or at some fixed future date. Obtaining debt funding for a business experiencing problems will require consideration of appropriate funding arrangements and evidence of the capacity to service and repay the debt being sought. Dealing with your financier in a crisis situation, including options and opportunities to refinance your business, are discussed in detail in Chapters 10 and 11.

There are funding options that provide some of the characteristics of both debt and equity. The issue of redeemable preference shares is one such funding option. Redeemable preference shares usually attract preferred dividends (payable only if the business is sufficiently profitable) and are redeemable at some future time or subject to some future conditions. They are not secured, and rank behind debt in a wind up. Convertible notes are another hybrid between debt and equity. Convertible notes attract regular interest payments but are usually subordinated to bank debt. The issuer of the convertible notes and/or the holder of the notes has the capacity, subject to specific conditions, to convert the notes into equity at some future time.

Sale of part of your business

The owners of businesses experiencing difficulties sometimes look to resolve their problems by selling part or all of the business as a going concern. Sale of the whole business is an exit strategy rather than a turnaround strategy. Exit strategies are discussed in Chapter 13.

In some cases, it will be possible to sell off part of the business. My experience has been that the tendency in these cases is to sell off the profitable business units, which are more sought after and will bring a higher price, rather than to sell the loss-making business units. The problem with this strategy is obvious.

The most likely buyers of your business will be your competitors. The sale process will inevitably involve the disclosure of information that may be used by your competitors to enhance their own business. Often, expressions of interest by competitors are only fishing expeditions in seeking out information for their own benefit. There are measures taken to prevent such activities by competitors but it is difficult to secure highly sensitive information in a business sale process. There is little more that can be done other than to seek confidentiality agreements and contractual restrictions on the use of information disclosed during a sale process to protect against these activities.

Sale of business assets

It is very common for businesses in trouble to sell off surplus assets to generate cash. Such strategies are legitimate turnaround strategies to the extent that they reduce costs by, for example, applying the cash from asset sales to debt reduction. Asset sales may also be used to generate cash to keep the business trading by supporting working capital or assisting the business to meet financial obligations. Asset sales for these purposes are more closely aligned with strategies designed to buy time.

9.   Your turnaround plan

So far you have identified the cause or causes of the problems, decided that you are the right person to manage the turnaround process, engaged an adviser (if you decide that is necessary), assessed your current position, identified the resources you have available, and examined and prioritised the threats facing your business. You can now prepare your turnaround plan. The purpose of your turnaround plan will be to guide your actions and provide a yardstick for measuring your performance towards your objectives. It is a practical and very important tool.

Your plan objectives

The first and most important element of your turnaround plan will be identifying and documenting your strategy objectives. These will obviously be directed at resolving the problems you have identified with your business. Your high-level objectives will probably look something like these:

- To stabilise the business while you implement your turnaround strategies.
- To turn the business around by fixing the causes of the current problems.
- To design and implement strategies to ensure the problems never occur again.

It is important that your strategy objectives provide a clear sight of where your turnaround plan is intended to take your business.

Strategy objectives should then be supported by measurable targets against which you may assess the performance of the turnaround plan. These targets will not only be quantitative measures but must also include timelines. So, the high-level objectives will have targets that will provide specific, measurable outcomes and timelines. As an example, in the case of a business where trading losses are causing the problems in the business, the high-level objective of fixing the causes of the current problems might incorporate targets such as:

- improving sales by 5% within three months, and by 10% within a year
- achieving a break-even profit result within six months (for example, by July 20XX) and consistently maintaining profitable trading thereafter, with a sustainable profit before tax of $40,000 per month (for example, by December 20XX)
- improving gross profit margins by 1% by increasing prices and reducing direct production costs within six months.

It is not sufficient to have a target that says "the business will become profitable". Although this defines the intention to make the business profitable, it does not identify the extent of the profits required or the time within which the business will become profitable. You cannot measure your success against this target because it has no time limit. A better way is to define the time and extent of the profit you are seeking to achieve, so this objective might read, "the business will make a trading profit every month from May 20XX onwards, and monthly profit will be a minimum of $50,000 by October 20XX". You will note that this objective does not attempt to define the processes or steps by which the business will achieve profitability. You can be more precise about the manner in which you will achieve your targets. For example, you can set out the steps by which the target above will be achieved – for instance, "this will be achieved by reducing headcount by one person per month from January 20XX; by renegotiating purchasing arrangements to reduce the cost of inputs by no less than 5% by March 20XX; and by increasing sales by 3% per month from February 20XX". The objective now defines a range of benchmarks to be achieved from as early as January 20XX, with monthly performance objectives across headcount, input costs, and sales that may be used to assess progress towards achieving the ultimate objectives of profitability by May 20XX and a profit of $50,000 per month by October 20XX.

Incorporating a range of targets with benchmarks that are progressive in nature will allow you to more closely and accurately assess the performance of your turnaround plan in a timely manner.

Documenting your turnaround plan

Your plan should be written down in a form that will make it easy to follow. Start with each objective and, underneath each objective, identify the specific targets to be met. Beneath each target, identify all of the tasks or actions that you believe are required to achieve that target. Then put each of these actions or tasks into a sequential order based on your view of their importance, which should be based on the likely impact the task will have on the successful completion of the turnaround. Identify those tasks that you consider critical to either the survival of the business or the success of the turnaround.

Let's consider an example. Say a creditor has started winding up action in court due to an unpaid bill. Stopping the creditor's wind-up action is clearly a critical activity because if the action is successful an administrator will be appointed to the business. So, the objective is to stop or defer the winding up action. One option is to pay the amount demanded by the creditor. Another is to negotiate payment terms with the creditor, subject to the court action being discontinued. Yet another option is to contest the winding up action in the court. This option will be much more complex than the first two options as it will require engaging a lawyer, preparing evidence to submit to the court, and possibly attending the court to give evidence. It may be that you decide to seek to negotiate payment terms with the creditor in the first instance and, failing that, to pay the amount owing. This course of action involves two steps; the first being to negotiate with the creditor, and the second being making a payment to the creditor (noting that the negotiation will almost invariably involve a payment to the creditor – hopefully for either a lesser amount or for the same amount payable over a longer period of time).

When you are making up the lists of tasks to be completed, you will need to identify dependencies – these are actions or tasks that are dependent upon the completion of another task before they can or will be commenced. The first task is known as a "precondition" or "precedent" to the task that follows. The following task is a "dependent" of the first task.

In some cases, you will find that there are a number of tasks that necessarily follow each other in a chain, as each of the tasks is a precondition to the next task (these tasks together make up a "group" of tasks). List these tasks together in order under the first task in the group and identify them as being related as preconditions by using a line or arrow to join each task to its following task or action. Some tasks will be preconditions to several other tasks or possibly even a precondition to an entire segment of the turnaround plan.

In the example of a creditor taking steps to initiate a winding up, your first task might be to assess if you have the capacity to pay the creditor before the wind-up application is heard by the court. Your second task, which will only be required if you decide not to pay the creditor, might be to try to negotiate a payment arrangement with the creditor. This task is a dependent of the first task because it only starts if the first task isn't completed (that is, if you don't pay the creditor). Your third task might be to contest the wind-up application in court. This task is a dependent of the second task as it is not required if the creditor agrees to a payment plan. Of course, defending the wind-up action in court might be your first task if you feel the need to contest the wind-up action in preference to the other options. Under this option (whether it is your first or third task) you will list all of the actions required to defend the wind-up action in court.

You will then need to assign each task an expected starting date. If you do not initially have a starting date for each task, then assign as a starting date the earliest date at which you believe the task will be commenced.

Now go through each task or action and estimate how much time will be required to complete that task or action. When you have completed this you will have a timetable for completion of all the tasks that are necessary for the successful implementation of your turnaround plan. Where there are dependent tasks or a group of tasks, the time taken to complete the last task will be the sum of the time taken to complete this task and all of its preconditions.

In the example we have been working through in this chapter, you might decide to start assessing if you can pay the creditor immediately and determine that it will take you a couple of days working through your cash flows to assess if you can pay the creditor. So, your start date is today and your completion date is the end of day two. Task 2 will start on day three, and you might allow another three days to agree a payment deal with the creditor. That means Task 2 will be completed by the end of day five. Task 3 will then start on day six. If your lawyer tells you it will take two weeks to prepare and lodge a defence for the court, then the preparation stage of Task 3 will be completed on day twenty. If the creditor has issued a statutory demand, you will have to lodge your defence with the court within 21 days, so you only have one day of contingency available in this group of tasks. In this instance, time will have to be closely managed or you will risk not meeting the deadline to lodge your defence with the court. That opportunity will be lost and you place your business at grave risk of being wound up by the court.

There will be circumstances where the available time is exceeded by the time required to complete all of the tasks in a group of tasks. Planning your task listings carefully will allow you to identify these circumstances in advance. There will be occasions where these expected time overruns place the success of your turnaround plan at risk. Where this occurs, you must resolve the threat by either finding a way to extend the available time, or reducing the time to complete some tasks in the group.

Critical tasks should be marked so that they are easily identifiable as the tasks to which you should give priority. As noted earlier, critical tasks are those that are critical to either the survival of the business or the success of the turnaround. Some tasks will be critical because they are essential to prevent actions by others that will cause your turnaround plan to fail. An example of this type of task would be action to prevent a creditor from taking wind-up action or to bring an end to wind-up action that has already been started by a creditor. Other tasks will be critical because they are essential to keep the business trading. Such tasks might include ensuring that staff are paid, stock or essential raw materials can be purchased, maturing debt facilities are extended or completing an order in a timely manner to maintain essential cash flow of the business. Completion of critical tasks are milestone events. They should be noted as such in your plan so that you can focus your attention on critical activities and the achievement of milestone events in the course of implementing your turnaround plan.

Implementing your turnaround plan

Prioritise, monitor, manage, review, and update

Your turnaround plan will have two critical elements that will each require effective and timely management. These elements are resources and relationships. The resources you will need to implement your plan will include cash, physical assets and people. The relationships you will need to manage in implementing your plan will be relationships with people both internal and external to the business.

Implementation of your turnaround plan will involve six key tasks:

1. **Prioritising** the allocation of resources to the tasks that need to be completed in accordance with the turnaround plan.
2. **Managing relationships** with internal and external stakeholders to complete the tasks set out in your turnaround plan and to avoid interference with, and/or maximise support for, the successful achievement of your plan.
3. **Monitoring** the completion of tasks and the achievement of targets and milestones in accordance with the turnaround plan.
4. **Reviewing the performance** of resources against their role and objectives in the turnaround plan.
5. **Identifying and responding** to any new issues or events that are impacting upon the turnaround plan.
6. **Updating** the turnaround plan as required.

Implementing a turnaround plan can be a difficult and often complex process. It will require commitment, time, effort, diplomacy, organisational skills, patience and, above all, perseverance.

One of the most important resources you will have to manage is your own time. You should clearly distinguish in your mind your role in implementing your turnaround plan from the role you have in actually managing the day-to-day activities of the business. It is a case of ensuring that, with respect to the turnaround plan, you are working "on" the business rather than "in" the business.

It is also important to recognise at the outset that no plan ever goes perfectly. There will be events that were not foreseen when the plan was prepared. You will need to modify and adapt the plan as these unforeseen circumstances arise.

Prioritising the allocation of resources

In preparing your turnaround plan, you will have identified critical tasks that have to be performed, and the time required to complete those tasks. This process will have identified the most important tasks that need to be completed. You will then need to consider how these critical tasks relate to each other and their relative significance to your turnaround plan so that you can prioritise the critical tasks. In some cases, the priority of the critical task will be elevated because of the threat it poses to the survival of the business. In other cases, the priority will be determined by the need to commence a task earlier than another task to meet a desired deadline or timetable.

The priority applied to resources will largely be driven by the priority applied to the various tasks that have to be performed under your turnaround plan. All of the tasks to be completed will require specific resources to be dedicated to the completion of that task. There is almost always a scarcity of resources when a business is experiencing serious problems, and there will almost certainly be conflicts between the available resources and the immediate need for those resources. With limited resources you will not be able to do everything that needs to be done when it needs to be done. Your role in implementing the turnaround plan will involve prioritising the tasks that must be performed, having regard to the objectives of the turnaround plan and the resources that you have available to you. In prioritising your resources, you will need to direct them to their most significant role in the turnaround process.

The success of your turnaround will be significantly impacted by your ability to manage the allocation of scarce resources to critical tasks.

The most common scarcity you will encounter is likely to be cash, although other resources may also be in short supply. These may include raw materials or finished stock (which are depleted generally because of a lack of cash to replenish them), and/or people. Important machinery may also be unavailable or operating at less than optimal capacity due to a need for repairs and maintenance.

It is likely that cash will also be the most difficult resource to prioritise because cash will be the resource that is most in demand and in shortest supply. The high level of demand for cash will be driven not only by the needs of the business but also by the demands of creditors for payment. Cash inflows will probably be lumpy, and there will be a tendency towards "oiling the squeaky wheel" by paying the creditors who complain the most without necessarily identifying them as being of the highest priority. It is essential that you stick to your plan and prioritise in accordance with achievement of your plan's objectives. This can be very challenging.

Managing relationships

Another important role that you will perform in implementing your turnaround plan (and perhaps the most significant) is the management of relationships.

There will be many voices of complaint, both internal and external, which will seek both your attention and the diversion of resources to sub-optimal roles.

Managing external relationships can be the most challenging role in any turnaround. Key external relationships will include suppliers, service providers, and taxation authorities (all of whom are also likely to be creditors), customers (debtors), and financiers. The difficulty in dealing with external relationships is that they are all different and each external relationship will be driven by different forces. Some will be favourably disposed to assist and/or support your business. Others will be totally dispassionate about your position. When you prioritise the allocation of your scarce resources, some creditors won't be paid when they want to be paid. The first challenge that you will face in managing external relationships will be identifying the attitude of the other party toward your circumstances and the level of threat they pose to the successful implementation of your turnaround plan.

Your bank is usually the most important external relationship you will have to manage. Chapter 11 is dedicated to discussing how to manage your relationship with your bank.

Internal stakeholders include staff and shareholders. There are added vulnerabilities with respect to staff in a business experiencing problems, as their loyalty will be tested by a combination of uncertainty about their future and the additional work stresses that will inevitably arise during the turnaround process. You will need to help them understand the importance of their role in the turnaround strategy and recognise their incremental efforts. Bring them along on the journey. They will appreciate being kept informed of your goals and your timetable. Share the successes and the setbacks of the turnaround strategy with them. Make them feel that they are part of the solution. However, always remember that they have their own financial obligations to meet and, unless you are the only employer in town who might employ them, they will have alternative employment options if they feel they are being pushed too hard or if they don't share your positive outlook for the success of your plan. Balancing your demands upon your staff with their capacity and their expectations will require careful consideration and, possibly, tailoring your demands to individual circumstances. Managing your people is further discussed in Chapter 12.

Monitoring the achievement of targets and milestones

Your turnaround plan represents a course of action that is designed to achieve specific objectives within defined timeframes. Your plan is a roadmap to your destination – which is the successful completion of the turnaround of your business. You should follow your roadmap closely and regularly monitor your progress towards your destination. This should be a disciplined process. It is of little benefit to have a turnaround plan unless you monitor the implementation of the plan to ensure that your progress accords with your expectations and objectives as set out in your plan. A detailed review of your progress should be undertaken at least monthly – and more often if your target dates are being missed. Focus on critical tasks first as these impact on other tasks and the ultimate achievement of your objectives. Be vigilant about the timing of the completion of critical tasks as time delays can have a material flow-on effect right through your turnaround plan and might ultimately be fatal if not carefully managed.

Reviewing the performance of resources against their role and objectives

You will have limited resources available to you to implement your turnaround plan, so you will need to manage them to ensure that you extract maximum value from what you have. As part of your regular reviews of your turnaround plan, you should assess the performance of resources against the tasks assigned to them, to determine whether the resources are achieving the outcomes you expected from them. It may also be that other tasks have emerged or priorities have changed in such a way that resources must be reallocated to alternative tasks. There will often be competing demand for the same resources. Successful implementation of the turnaround plan involves ensuring your resources are always efficiently and effectively allocated.

Identifying and responding to new issues or events

No plan ever goes exactly as expected, so be prepared for unforeseen events. In most cases you will come across other events that may impede or delay your turnaround plan. Such events will typically emerge as a result of unforeseen actions by third parties (such as creditors, suppliers, competitors, employees or regulators). Sometimes, you may identify tasks that have been missed or overlooked when you were preparing your plan. New tasks may emerge (possibly in the course of completing other tasks) that may be necessary for the successful implementation of your plan.

Updating your turnaround plan

Your plan will need to be regularly reviewed and adjusted, at least once a month. Update your task listing by removing those tasks that have been successfully completed, amending the timeframe for completion of other tasks as required, and adding any new tasks that have emerged since the last update. Document new tasks by adding them to the turnaround plan in the same manner as other tasks, prioritising any of the new tasks that might be critical, establishing completion dates and, where applicable, milestone dates for each task.

Your turnaround plan will be a dynamic document that continually evolves as you progress through the turnaround process.

10. Managing cash flow

Managing cash flow is a critical element of turning your business around. The more serious the difficulties your company is experiencing, the more critical cash flow management will become. This chapter is dedicated to helping you identify the strategy options available to manage your cash flow and generate more cash for your business.

Almost every business that is experiencing difficulties will experience cash stress. It is the most common symptom of trouble and one of the most serious. In the short-term, it is the most important symptom, and one that demands immediate and ongoing attention and action. A business experiencing a shortage of cash struggles to pay, or is unable to pay, its operating expenses when they are due to be paid. Failure to pay some expenses of a business, such as wages and salaries, can have potentially immediate and serious consequences as staff become immediately uncertain and demoralised and may withdraw their labour until paid. Delays in payment of wages will also quickly attract the attention of labour unions and the government authorities. Although there may generally be some leeway in the timing available for payment of other expenses of the business, failure to pay creditors or financing obligations will ultimately lead to creditors or your bank taking action that will result in the appointment of administrators to the business – or its liquidation.

The cash cycle and working capital

There are a number of steps that can be taken to improve cash flow within your business. Cash is one element of working capital and the "cash cycle" is a subsection of the trading cycle. Understanding and managing the cash cycle of your business can be an effective way of generating and sustaining an improved cash position in your business and a relatively quick and easy source of additional cash.

The cash cycle

In any business, cash generation is a cyclical activity. Cash is first invested in buying stock, manufacturing a product (creating stock), or supplying a service. The stock or service is then sold to customers and an invoice is raised, at which time the stock or service has been converted into a debt owed by the customers of the business (retailers generally get paid immediately or within a couple of days). When these debts are paid by the customers of the business the debt is converted to cash in the business and the cycle starts again.

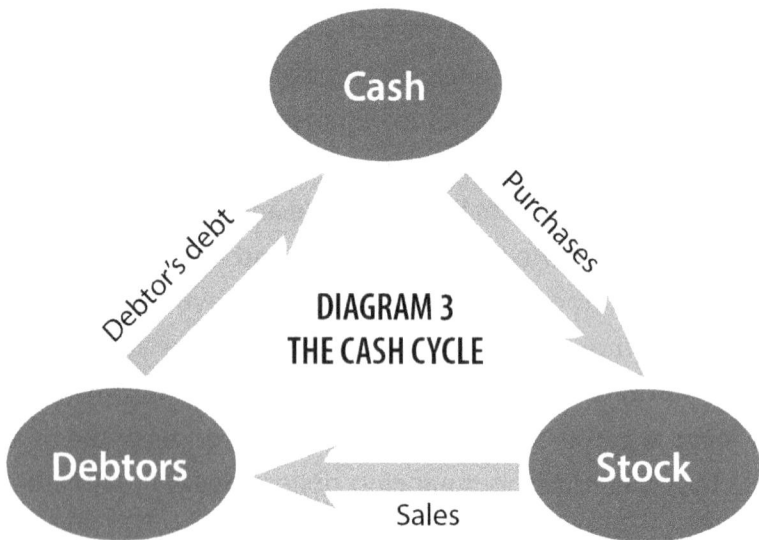

Cash

Debtor's debt

Purchases

DIAGRAM 3
THE CASH CYCLE

Debtors

Stock

Sales

If the business is profitable, there is more cash remaining at the end of the cash cycle than when the cash cycle started, and the cash resources of the business will grow. Conversely, if the business is making trading losses the amount of cash remaining at the end of the cash cycle will be less than it was at the beginning.

Reducing the amount of time cash is locked up in stock or debtors can have a significant, cumulative benefit to the cash position of your business. Faster cycling of cash will reduce the amount of debt required to fund working capital, and save on financing costs. Faster cycling of cash also reduces risk in the business.

Sources of cash

When a business starts out, the initial source of cash is money provided by the business proprietor (equity). This start-up equity can be supplemented with borrowings (debt funding) from a financier. Once a business is trading, the primary source of cash flows into the business is by way of payments from customers for sales made in the normal course of business, and cash revolves in and out of the business via the cash cycle. Funds may also be provided to the business from outside of the cash cycle via additional loans from financiers, from the proceeds of asset sales, and/or by further equity subscriptions from shareholders. Equity and debt are external sources of funds for the business. These are often difficult sources to tap when a business is in trouble.

There are two sides to effective cash flow management – getting cash into the business and reducing the rate at which cash goes out of the business.

There are a number of opportunities to raise additional cash or accelerate cash turnover to help your business through difficult times. These opportunities are both internal and external to the business. Internal opportunities to raise additional cash are derived from management of the elements of the working capital of the business or, alternatively, from the sale of assets, and include:

- sale of surplus or redundant stock

- reducing debtors by collecting debts faster or "factoring" debtors
- asset sales.

External opportunities to raise additional cash are derived from sources outside of your business and include:

- borrowings from banks, financiers, family, friends
- seeking additional equity funding or loans from directors, shareholders or third parties.

Keeping cash in your business

There are also opportunities to retain cash in your business longer (reducing or slowing cash outflows).

Cash flows out of the business to purchase raw materials, pay labour, purchase stock, pay overheads, pay business taxes, and pay interest on debt. Cash also goes out of the business for non-operating outlays such as to purchase assets, repay loans, and to pay dividends to shareholders.

A business that is having cash flow problems has a number of opportunities to either reduce the amount of cash going out of the business or slow the rate at which cash flows out of the business. These opportunities can be either permanent reductions in cash outflows or short-term opportunities to retain cash in the business longer than normal.

Permanent reductions in cash outflows can result from:

- negotiating lower prices for business inputs
- reducing staff numbers
- reducing overhead expenses
- reducing or ceasing the payment of dividends
- negotiating lower debt interest charges.

Opportunities to retain cash in the business longer include:

- delaying payments to creditors/improving terms of payment to creditors
- timing purchases to maximise the time between purchase and payment
- suspension or reduction of repayments on loans by paying only interest
- extending the term of loans to reduce regular instalments
- deferral of asset finance payments or extending the term of the finance facility
- deferral of tax obligations or making arrangements to pay tax over time.

Working capital

The working capital of the business is a measure of the ability of the company to generate cash from internal sources. It is the sum of the assets of the business that can be readily turned into cash (being cash, stock and debtors) less the short-term financial obligations of the business (creditors/payables and short-term loan repayments due).

The mix of current assets making up the working capital of a business will vary from time to time as the business moves through its trading cycle. A business with a positive working capital position (that is, where the current assets exceed the short-term financial obligations) has the capacity to fund the trading activities of the business without the need for external funding, provided that the working capital position is effectively managed. A business with a negative working capital position will have greater difficulty in meeting its short-term obligations, and faces the prospect of continuing cash stress as it cannot internally generate sufficient cash to meet those obligations in a timely manner. Such a business requires either an injection of external funds or very astute working capital management (or both) to avoid cash flow difficulties.

Managing working capital

Effective working capital management is the most accessible, simplest, and most valuable contribution you can make to your business. It will improve the cash flow of the business and maximise the opportunities and time available to turn your business around. In the longer term, effective working capital management practices will also reduce the capital requirements of the business (therefore improving the return on equity), and improve profitability by reducing the level of external debt required to fund working capital.

Poor working capital management is often the cause of businesses experiencing cash flow problems. How you manage each of the elements that make up the working capital of your business will significantly influence the cash position of your business.

In normal times, managers generally seek to turn over stock at a rate which will generate an adequate gross profit, collect monies from debtors in accordance with their normal payment terms, pay creditors in accordance with the creditor's payment terms, and make short-term loan repayments in accordance with the relevant loan documentation. In many businesses, over time, the discipline around the management of stock levels and collection of debtors can wane. Although assets such as stock and debtors are considered to be current assets (capable of being realised in the current accounting period) poor management of these assets can result in cash being "locked up" in these assets. This situation, known as "cash lock-up", occurs when your business has obsolete or slow-moving stock that cannot be readily sold or when you have slow-paying or delinquent debtors. The time that cash spends locked up in each of these elements of your working capital can be managed. Stock can be turned over quickly or slowly and debtors can be collected quickly or slowly.

Outlays can be similarly managed to reduce the rate at which cash flows out of the business. Creditors can be paid promptly or slowly. Short-term loan repayments can be renegotiated so they are reduced or suspended, to ease the burden on cash flows.

You need to review each of these elements and revise your stock management, debtor collection, creditor payment, and financing arrangements to keep cash flow positive and ensure the survival of the business.

The strict discipline required around working capital management is one of the key differences between managing a business in normal circumstances and managing a business that is in trouble. Adopting new practices necessary where working capital management is critical to survival can be difficult for many managers. It is often necessary to stretch business relationships, chase up debtor payments, seek forbearance, and ask for help. Hard conversations and actions are required that can be stressful and can damage pride. It is often very hard to admit to your suppliers, staff and customers that your business needs their support. It is common for managers to resort to easier options, rather than swallowing their pride, such as increasing debt (where the capacity to increase debt exists) to cover cash shortfalls, arguing that the alternative strategies may have negative effects on the business. While in some instances that may be true (usually as a result of poor communication or an existing lack of trust) increasing debt will only increase the risk of failure and add to the cash stress if the underlying problems are not remedied quickly. Effective working capital management is the cheapest and quickest source of cash for a business experiencing cash flow problems.

There are other options available which you may also wish to consider, and these are discussed later in this chapter. However, the simple fact is that effective working capital management is important to every business and critical to any business experiencing cash stress.

Stock

A very common way of raising cash quickly is by discounting surplus, slow-moving or redundant stock. The most common process by which this is achieved is via a sale where the price of the stock is reduced for quick sale. This process can often result in a significant amount of cash being raised in a short period of time and with minimal impact on the business. The extent of the discounting will be a function of the desperation of the cash need, the desirability of the discounted stock, and the price that will make your customers buy the product now.

Other options to reduce stock include offering bulk lines of stock to individual customers (although this will often result in a decline in future orders from those customers and an adjustment to their price expectations), auctioning the excess stock (online auctions are very popular these days) or seeking to return excess stock to your supplier for a refund or credit.

Whatever strategy you choose, it will usually be necessary to offer material discounts to trigger sales. Do not be afraid to sell slow-moving or obsolete stock below cost if that is necessary to generate much-needed cash.

Be wary of reducing or heavily discounting popular stock lines unless you are overstocked in these lines or desperate for cash, as this will have a larger impact on future sales, profitability and customer expectations. Discounting popular stock lines will improve short-term cash flows as a result of customers bulk buying when prices are down; but they will then refrain from purchasing the items again due to holding adequate supply or in anticipation of further sales at reduced prices. This will not only result in volatile sales but will also have an adverse effect on gross profit margins.

Moreover, avoid reducing stock levels by running down or not replacing popular stock lines. The ability of your business to maintain its sales is dependent upon having sufficient stock available to meet customer demand, so it is a delicate balancing act to reduce stock without reducing the capacity of the business to trade. This can become a downward spiral as a reduction in popular stock lines results in reduced sales, which results in less cash flow, which results in reduced capacity to purchase stock, which results in reduced stock, and so on.

In the absence of a critical cash need, stock reduction as a method of raising cash should, at least initially, be limited to surplus, slow-moving or redundant stock. In determining what is surplus stock, you will need to consider your ability to restock quickly if and when the business picks up.

Debtors

Debtors are the customers of your business who owe your business money. If you operate a business that sells to other businesses, your customers will expect you to allow them time to pay for the goods and services you sell to them. On the other hand, you will also expect your suppliers and service providers to provide you with credit. The exceptions to these arrangements are retailers and service providers that provide services directly to consumers. These businesses will normally be paid when their goods are sold or when their service is provided to the customer.

Your products or services represent an investment of your resources and your money – whether by way of materials, staff wages, rent, insurance, delivery costs, or any number of other business costs. The goods or services you sell to your customers have cost you money, time and effort, but you do not get this money back, or any return on the money, time and effort invested, until your customer pays you. When you allow time for a customer to pay, you are in effect lending them money and you are taking on credit risk, just like a bank. Yet few small to medium businesses take the time to understand, or try to manage, the risks associated with lending money to their customers.

If your customer never pays you for your goods or services you will lose all the money, time and effort you have invested in those goods or services. If you derive a large proportion of your business income from one customer, then the failure of that customer could be fatal to your business (this is known as "concentration risk" because a large proportion of your income is concentrated on one or a few customers). It should not surprise you to learn that many businesses fail when one of their major customers fails to pay them. The collapse of a substantial business can have a flow-on effect, and potentially be fatal, to many businesses that traded with the collapsed business.

There is, however, a much more common problem relating to customer payments that very often afflicts troubled businesses – late or slow payment by debtors. If your customers do not pay you before you have to pay your suppliers, staff, and service providers for the resources you have used to produce the goods or services sold to them, then you have to finance those costs until you get paid. That means you have to take on additional debt or come up with additional equity to fund your business. Recall the impact on Jack's Furniture (Chapter 1) when his customer delayed payment to Jack from 30 days after delivery to 60 days. The amount of cash he was required to invest or borrow increased by 50%. When you have to fund business costs as a result of slow payment by your customers, your business is incurring additional costs (such as interest on your debt), your cash flow is restricted, and your profits are reduced. If a large amount of debts owed to your business by your customers are locked up due to slow payment, it can cost you thousands of dollars each year. You are effectively financing the working capital of your customers' businesses. Equally importantly, the money you have tied up in debtors could be used to reduce your debt or to grow your business. In addition, the extent to which your business is exposed to credit risk is directly proportional to the number of debtors who owe you money and the amount of money owed to you by debtors. This risk increases substantially as the age of a debt increases because of the increasing likelihood that they have their own cash flow problem.

Many small and medium business owners consider they have no choice but to accept slow payments because they risk losing the customer if they either don't allow them to pay slowly or complain about slow payment. There is an element of truth in this view, particularly when you are dealing with larger businesses. Some customers will take their business elsewhere if they are forced to pay on time. On the other hand, allowing your customers to extend their payment terms can be fatal to your business as your business may become unable to meet its financial commitments when they fall due. Some large businesses exploit the vulnerable negotiating position of their small and medium suppliers by extending their payment terms when they are trying to conserve cash. In the case of large businesses, this is a cheap way of financing their business using your money. Government departments can also be slow payers but this is generally either because they have inefficient bureaucratic payment processes or because they have exhausted their current allocation of funds.

Whether or not to accept slow payment or extended payment terms from your customers is a management decision – but it should be your decision. Although there is no right or wrong answer, it is important to make an informed decision on the basis of what is best for your business. I have seen some businesses struggle for years after losing the business of a key customer who was refused extended payment terms and, in one or two cases, I have seen businesses fail for this reason. However, I have seen many more good businesses brought to their knees by customers who are slow to pay.

One of the easiest and quickest ways to raise money is by accelerating the collection of monies owed to the business by debtors.

Collecting money from debtors

There are a number of ways for a business to accelerate the collection of money from debtors. The strategies you adopt will depend upon the individual circumstances of your business, your relationship with your customers, and the payment history of your customers. If you are dealing with customers who have historically paid you in accordance with your normal payment terms, consider the following strategy options:

ASK YOUR CUSTOMERS TO PAY PROMPTLY

You can write to all of your customers and simply ask them for prompt payment. Alternatively, get on the phone to your larger customers and politely ask them if they would please pay your outstanding invoices immediately and future invoices promptly. There is no shame in acknowledging that you need the cash to meet your commitments, and most of your suppliers will have experienced similar circumstances themselves at some time. It is preferable that these requests be made personally rather than via a staff member. A personal request from you is much more likely to be successful as it is you who has the relationship with your customers, and your customers will respect the fact that you have taken the time to call them personally and explain the circumstances of the request. It is likely that, provided you have a good relationship with your customer, they will accommodate your request. Don't let your pride get in the way of the survival of your business.

OFFER CUSTOMERS AN INCENTIVE TO PAY PROMPTLY

It is very common for businesses to offer their customers prompt payment discounts. These discounts provide a financial incentive for customers to pay the invoices ahead of normal payment terms. Most large businesses and government departments seek to take advantage of early payment discounts when the discount exceeds the cost of funds. For example, a large business that normally pays on 60-day terms would be incentivised to pay on 30-day terms if a 2% early payment discount was offered, as this would be equivalent to a return of 24% per annum on the funds used to pay the invoice.

INVOICE YOUR GOODS AND SERVICES IN A TIMELY MANNER

Make sure that your business is invoicing customers at the earliest opportunity. If you are able to invoice your customer at the end of the month rather than the beginning of the next month, you will reduce the payment timeframe by almost a month. Where the supply of goods or services extends over a period exceeding one month, look for opportunities to make progress claims on a monthly basis at the end of each month rather than waiting until all the goods or services have been provided. Consider, for example, part deliveries for larger orders.

INCORPORATE PROGRESS PAYMENTS INTO CONTRACTS AND STANDARD TERMS OF SUPPLY

When negotiating new contracts, seek to incorporate progress claims on a monthly basis into the contract. Consider amending your standard terms of supply to include the option to invoice the customer on a monthly basis where completion of the customer order extends over more than one billing cycle.

INCORPORATE UP-FRONT PAYMENTS INTO CONTRACTS AND STANDARD TERMS OF SUPPLY

Where the opportunity presents you should consider requiring up-front payments, particularly where the customer order requires a substantial investment in materials. Your ability to negotiate up-front payments will be dependent on a number of factors including your relationship with the customer, the importance and urgency of the order, and the customer's policies. It never hurts to ask.

CONSIDER DEBTOR FINANCE

Another strategy to raise funds from the debtor book of your business is to secure a debtor finance (or "factoring") facility. Under a debtor finance facility, the financier buys the debt owed to your business for its face value less interest and fees. When an invoice is raised, the financier pays a proportion of the value of invoice (often 70% to 80%) giving the business access to these funds immediately. When the invoice is ultimately paid the financier retains the funds advanced, plus their interest and fees, and the balance of the invoice amount is released to the business.

There are two types of debtor finance – "disclosed" facilities, where your customer knows the debt has been sold and "undisclosed", where the fact that the debt has been sold is not disclosed to your customer. With disclosed facilities your customers are normally directed to make invoice payments to the account of the financier.

Debtor finance facilities are most commonly available to firms that provide recurrent supplies or services to other businesses. Financiers are less comfortable providing debtor finance against contract progress payments where there is a risk that the customer will not pay if the subsequent terms of the contract are not fully satisfied. Such circumstances exist in, for example, construction contracts.

Debtor finance will provide a one-off boost to cash when the facility is first drawn, by immediately turning up to 80% of the current debtor book into cash. However, be aware that, if you have other existing finance in your business, your current lender probably has a charge over the debtors of the business. You will need to obtain their written agreement to release their security over the debtors of the business before you will be able to put a debtor finance facility in place.

CHASE UP OVERDUE DEBTS

Collecting money from customers who have a history of being slow payers or who are overdue in paying their invoices requires a different approach. You will need to consider the importance of the customer relationship to your business and make a judgement about the sensitivity of the customer before deciding the strategies you will adopt.

Nevertheless, remember that it is your money that they are holding onto once their payment is beyond your normal payment terms. You are, in effect, providing funds to their business and supporting their working capital to the detriment of your own working capital position. You are not in the business of banking or financing your customers. Taking positive steps to collect overdue debts is, therefore, an entirely reasonable and appropriate strategy to adopt, particularly when your business is in need of cash. Many customers are slow to make payment to their suppliers because their suppliers accept slow payment. Customers become accustomed to paying late without penalty and so it becomes part of their normal practice. Asking them to pay on time may result in a change in their behaviour, although it is likely that they will protest the change in the way things have previously been done. Do not feel guilty about asking for payment in accordance with your normal payment terms. These are the terms upon which you supply goods or services to your customers and it is your customer who is in breach of the terms upon which your goods or services were supplied. If you are not comfortable with chasing overdue debts personally then consider employing an experienced person to chase up overdue debtors or engaging a collection agent. However, be aware that being chased by a debt collector will probably upset your customer and damage your relationship with them. It is better to make the call yourself if it is to a customer you are keen to retain.

CONSIDER ENFORCEMENT ACTION

If asking your customers to pay overdue accounts immediately does not result in a positive outcome, you may need to consider taking action to recover the debt. This can be, on occasions, a difficult decision, particularly where the customer is one of long standing or is a significant contributor to your sales. It is a judgement call for management to make, but you need to consider the alternative outcomes. If the customer is one of long standing who is a consistently slow payer and who refuses to accelerate payment upon request, it is likely that you will continue to tolerate their slow payment (although you might consider adjusting pricing to reflect the additional cost to your business). Similarly, if the customer in question represents a significant part of your sales you may decide to continue to tolerate slow payment. However, bear in mind that a customer who pays slowly may be harbouring their own cash flow stresses and may represent a higher risk of non-payment.

If you decide to pursue enforcement action there are several options available:

- Engage a professional debt collector to seek to collect the debt on your behalf. There will obviously be a cost in using the services of a professional debt collector but it will save you the stress of engaging the customer in difficult conversations and the time required to prepare letters of demand.

- Sell the debt to a professional debt collector. This may not be an option for many businesses, but in some cases professional debt collection firms will purchase overdue debts from businesses at a substantial discount and take on the collection risk themselves. This is a common practice when numerous small consumer debts are involved such as credit cards or hire purchase debts.

- Take legal action to collect the debt. There are invariably legal options in all jurisdictions for businesses to collect unpaid debts. Although the process will vary from jurisdiction to jurisdiction, it will generally involve initially serving a demand for payment upon the customer and, if that demand is not satisfied within a specified period of time (usually 21 days), allowing an application to the court to be made for an administrator to be appointed to the defaulting business. This can be a very forceful and productive process if the customer has the capacity to pay. Where the customer is unable to pay, it can be a relatively costly way of securing little by way of return. It is generally a last-resort process because it will either result in a substantial deterioration in the relationship with the customer or in their ultimate demise. There are legal firms that specialise in debt collection action and it is often more cost-effective to use a specialist firm. Take the time when you first engage with your legal advisers to understand the process and the costs involved. It is not unusual for the customer who is being sued to allege that there is a bona fide dispute over the debt as a way of delaying the appointment of administrators to their business. If they are successful in arguing that a bona fide dispute exists, the debt collection process can become considerably protracted and more costly.

It is timely to note that many businesses that have failed have continued to supply or service customers who have been slow to pay them for an extended period of time, only to find that they have ultimately lost a substantial amount of money and that their losses could have been considerably reduced if they had responded to the slow payment behaviour earlier. If you have customers whose payment behaviour has slowed materially, be wary about continuing to extend additional credit. Contact them to find out why the payments have slowed or investigate the causes by doing a credit check or talking to their other customers. Remember that you are not in the business of financing the businesses of your customers outside of normal trading terms.

Asset sales

Another useful strategy for raising cash is to sell off surplus assets. Most businesses, over time, accumulate assets that are no longer used in the business or that are used only infrequently. There are also often assets within businesses where an equivalent asset can be hired without a substantial cost penalty which can make asset ownership unnecessary.

It is important that your expectations are realistic and achievable. You are only fooling yourself if you have unrealistic expectations, either in terms of the prices that you might achieve for the assets or in terms of the time it will take to sell them. If there is urgency or time pressure on asset sales you must recognise that it may be necessary to discount the assets to achieve a quick sale.

SALE AND LEASEBACK OF BUSINESS PREMISES

One very common asset that can be leased instead of owned is business premises. It is a normal practice for businesses to sell the premises they occupy and lease them back from the purchaser to generate cash to fund operating expenses or business growth. This is known as "sale and leaseback". Ownership of a business premises is normally pursued as an asset accumulation strategy by the owners of businesses. It is rarely a primary function of the business to own land and buildings, nor is it necessary for the effective operation of the business (with some exceptions). Be aware, however, that the sale and leaseback of property can take some time.

SALE AND LEASEBACK OF PLANT AND/OR EQUIPMENT

Sale and leaseback is sometimes an available option for plant and equipment, particularly for relatively new, high-value, mobile plant and equipment. Fixed or specialised plant and equipment can be more problematic and less attractive for a financier to purchase and leaseback, unless the business is long-established and financially sound. You will need to invest more time and effort into finding a financier willing to purchase and leaseback fixed plant and equipment.

PARTIAL SALE OF THE BUSINESS

Where a business has multiple trading divisions, you might consider selling off part of the business. This process involves selling severable components of the business rather than selling a share in the total business by raising equity (which is covered later). Partial sale of the business can be a useful method of moving out of less profitable parts of the business or parts of the business that have high overheads or carry higher risks relative to the return they generate. Of course, these parts of the business will be less saleable than the more profitable, higher margin parts of the business. Although it may become essential to sell off profitable elements of the business, be careful not to leave yourself with those parts of the business that will simply become a burden in years to come.

SALE OF PERSONAL ASSETS

Small business owners might also consider if they have surplus personal assets that can be sold to generate cash that can be invested in the business.

Raising cash for your business externally

Creditors

The most readily accessible and most commonly tapped source of external financing for a business are the creditors of the business. Unlike other sources of funding, creditors provide cash to your business when you delay paying them. The effect of delaying payment to your creditors is to retain cash within the business that might otherwise have gone out of the business. As a result, for the period that payment is deferred, there is additional cash available within your business that might be deployed to meet critical short-term expenses to keep the business afloat.

Most creditors will tolerate some delay in payment when they are dealing with a customer they trust or an important customer of their business. However, it is important not to destroy your credibility with your creditors by abusing the credit they provide to your business. Delaying payment beyond acceptable terms will inevitably result in creditors ceasing to supply your business and, ultimately, in creditors taking legal action to recover their debt.

Delaying payment to creditors (or "stretching" your creditors) can provide significant incremental cash flow to your business in the short-term. Remember that the creditors will ultimately have to be paid, and that you need to have a strategy that will position your business to be able to pay your creditors before they begin taking legal action to recover their debts. In many instances it will be possible to negotiate later payment by discussing your circumstances, explaining your strategies to resolve the short-term issues confronting your business, and requesting forbearance from your creditors. When you do negotiate for more favourable payment terms with your suppliers, it is important that you honour whatever commitments you give in terms of the timing of the delayed payments.

Failure to honour your commitments will undermine your credibility and result in the withdrawal of whatever favourable terms you have been able to secure. It is also more likely to trigger earlier legal action because your suppliers will become more concerned about the financial position of your business and your ability to pay them. In some instances, putting your suppliers on notice of your circumstances may cause them to withdraw credit terms to protect their interests. As with many decisions made in the course of a business turnaround, you will be required to exercise your judgement in deciding whether to request forbearance up-front from your suppliers.

It is common for businesses to stretch their creditors by simply starting to make payments to creditors more slowly than they have in the past. This strategy is usually preferred over negotiating slower payment terms because business owners are reluctant to acknowledge to their suppliers that they are experiencing difficulties or to ask for help. This approach carries greater risks because it is undertaken without the knowledge or consent of the suppliers, some of whom may be expected to react poorly to the change in payment behaviours. It is more difficult to anticipate the response of your suppliers in these circumstances, and to predict if and when a supplier may take legal action to recover its debt. Having said that, most suppliers will prefer less drastic measures in the first instance, such as chasing up payment by phone followed by correspondence from the supplier's lawyer before legal action is taken.

In most jurisdictions there are statutory prohibitions around incurring liabilities to third parties (including suppliers) when the business is insolvent. In general terms, a business is insolvent if it cannot pay its bills as and when they are due to be paid. In some circumstances you may be personally liable to the supplier for debts incurred when the business is insolvent. You may also be guilty of a criminal offence in some jurisdictions. New purchases from creditors should, therefore, only be undertaken where you are clearly able to demonstrate the intended source of repayment and that that source of repayment is genuine and adequate to meet the liabilities incurred.

Stretching creditors is also the most cost-effective external source of funding for your business as it is generally without additional cost. Some creditors will impose penalties for late payment and you should familiarise yourself with the terms upon which your supplier has agreed to provide goods or services to your business.

Options for managing payments to specific groups of creditors are discussed in Chapter 7.

On the downside, extending payment terms to your creditors will result in an increase in the total amount of creditors being carried by your business and the overall liabilities of your business will increase. Moreover, carrying a significant number of stretched creditors increases the commitment of management to creditors (and the more creditors are stretched the greater the management burden becomes). More time must be spent handling difficult conversations and massaging relationships to keep your creditors at bay and avoid legal action. Keeping your creditors as stretched as possible also increases the risk of legal action being implemented and/or credit defaults being recorded against your business. Stretching your creditors may also make your business less attractive to financiers. Like all turnaround strategy options, stretching creditors is a balancing act between maximising cash retention in your business, maintaining access to the goods and services needed by your business, and avoiding legal action against your business.

Purchases

Another way of maximising the amount of cash in your business is to manage the timing of your purchases so as to extend the time between purchasing goods and paying for them. Buying stock, supplies or services on credit early in the month means that you can effectively extend the amount of time before you have to pay your supplier, by up to a month. Defer deliveries of stock, goods, and services until the beginning of each month and try to make this part of your regular routine if possible.

Debt

Debt is another common source of external funding for your business when it needs additional cash. Increasing your borrowing is an appropriate strategy where the business is capable of supporting the servicing and repayment of the additional debt. It is often the case with businesses that are experiencing difficulties that they are, in fact, losing money, and adding an additional debt burden may only exacerbate the problem. If you are in this position, consider any decision to seek to borrow more money carefully. Make sure you know how you are going to pay the interest and how you are going to pay back the increased debt before you commit. There are circumstances where borrowing money is an appropriate strategy for a business in trouble. These include situations where the problems are caused by short-term or one-off issues that have been resolved or will, with some certainty, be resolved in the short-term. There should also be a high degree of certainty that the business will return to profitability and will be able to meet its commitments, including the additional debt, going forward. Another circumstance where debt is appropriate is where there is a clearly defined program of asset sales and those asset sales will provide sufficient funds to clear the debt within a reasonable period of time. Be careful, if you need asset sales to repay debt, that your expectations in terms of sale prices and timing are realistic and achievable.

If your business is struggling for profitability and/or cash flow, borrowing money may not be easy. If your financier does a proper analysis of the financial circumstances of your business they may well decide (and, in fact, they probably should decide) not to provide any additional debt funding, on the basis that the business currently lacks the capacity to service and repay the debt.

You can make a pretty quick assessment of your capacity to borrow money by asking yourself three questions and objectively and honestly looking at the answers to those questions. Those three questions are:

1. Do I have a sound history of meeting my financing obligations in a timely manner? If you have a poor credit history it will be much harder to borrow money, particularly when your business is in trouble. Answering "yes" to this question will be problematic for many businesses that are experiencing problems, because it is often the case that loan repayments are missed when cash flow becomes tight.

2. Does my business generate sufficient cash, above the money needed to meet its operating expenses, to allow it to pay interest on the additional debt I am seeking? The ability to service debt is becoming paramount to credit decisions in the modern era. The days of mainstream banks lending purely against the value of assets provided as security ("asset lending") are disappearing. While there are still lenders who will do asset lending, they are generally not mainstream banks and are usually at the more expensive end of the spectrum.

3. Can I clearly demonstrate where the money to repay the debt will come from and when I will be able to repay the debt? Your lender will obviously be interested in how and when the debt is going to be repaid. If the debt is going to be repaid from normal trading it will be necessary to demonstrate, with some certainty, that trading will reach the levels that you are relying on to generate sufficient cash flow to repay the debt over time. If you are relying upon asset sales to be able to repay the debt, you will need to be able to demonstrate that the assets will realise the prices you are expecting and that you will be able to

achieve the sale of those assets within the required timeframe. It is important not to place unrealistic values on assets. If the asset sales are subject to time pressure there may be a need to sell them below the value that could be achieved where there was unlimited time to sell them.

SOURCES OF DEBT FUNDING

If you do decide to seek additional debt there are a number of possible sources you might consider.

Your existing bank or financiers

If you have an existing (and sound) relationship with your bank or any other financiers then these should be your first port of call when you are seeking additional debt funding. In Chapter 11 there is a detailed discussion of how to manage your banking relationships, including strategies to seek additional funding from your bank.

Other banks

The finance industry is a very competitive one and it is likely that any approach for funding will be well received, in the first instance, by other banks. It is generally the rule that new customers are sought after by banks but, on the other hand, new customers will often be subject to a greater degree of scrutiny in the course of lending decisions. Given that a business in distress may be unattractive to its current bankers it is prudent to check out all alternative opportunities rather than relying on a single potential source of debt funding. Casting your net wide will maximise your chances of success and banks will be a cheaper source of finance than the following alternatives.

Second-tier lenders

There are a variety of financial institutions that may also be willing to provide funding to your business. They will range from mutual funds to credit unions to finance companies that specialise in specific types of lending. Most of these organisations will either cater to specific markets (for example, agriculture, manufacturing or service industries) or provide specific financing products such as asset finance, debt finance or trade finance. It is important to ensure that you pitch your business to a lender that is willing to lend into your market segment and is capable of providing the sort of funding you require. Be careful not to waste your time and effort with a lender where your business is outside of their target market segments or the products you are seeking are not within the ambit of their product mix.

Government agencies

Some government agencies offer support in the form of loans or grants to assist businesses. Often these loans are designed to support specific industries through restructuring or expansion. They may be available to facilitate or encourage specific outcomes (such as employment). On occasions, governments make debt funding available to businesses in specific industries that are experiencing difficulties as a result of natural disasters (droughts, storms, earthquakes, and similar catastrophic natural events) or changes to government regulations.

Loans or grants from government agencies may not be the complete solution to your funding needs, however, if you meet their qualifying criteria they may provide useful support or assistance through difficult times.

Family and friends

One of the most common sources of debt funding for businesses experiencing problems is the family and friends of the proprietors of the business. The most frequently tapped family relationship is that of the parents of the proprietors, who are often retired but willing to provide cash support or additional security to support the business of a child. Siblings and family friends are also frequently called upon for urgent financial support.

Regrettably, from my experience many of these loans never get repaid. They are sometimes the source of conflict between family members, and can lead to the breakup of longstanding relationships. The simple reason for this common outcome is that family and friends almost always lend on the strength of the relationship without conducting appropriate enquiries as to the circumstances of the business or its capacity to repay the debt. Even if they do make some enquiry, they are rarely skilled in lending risk assessment. Based on the risk of damage to family and friends' finances and relationships, my advice would be to avoid loans from family and friends if you can, although I am aware that they are often the only source of funds where the credit worthiness of the business has been impugned.

If you do consider family and friends as a source of funding for your business, be careful to consider the implications or possible consequences if your business is unable to repay the loan. Desperation can lead us to make poor decisions that may have long-term, unwanted, and sometimes very dire consequences both for you as a borrower and for your family and/or friends. I have seen parents lose their homes as a result of guaranteeing the business debts of their children. I have seen the lives and relationships of parents, siblings and friends severely impacted as a result of their blind generosity in supporting troubled businesses.

The message here is that it is important for all concerned that you explain the circumstances of your business plainly, and make them aware of the risks you are asking them to take. You should make it very clear that there is a chance the business may never be able to pay them back. Even if you are confident you will be able to repay the debt or if you have an alternative source of repayment from your own resources, you should be totally frank about your position and the risks involved to your family or friends. Remember, these people usually do not have the sophistication to properly assess or understand the risks they are taking on when they lend money to your business. They are relying on your goodwill and your integrity in taking money from them.

It is also prudent to document the terms of any loan arrangement with family and friends so there is no misunderstanding in the future about what arrangements were intended. Confusion or misunderstanding around the terms of the loan can be just as damaging to relationships as failure to repay the loan.

Another circumstance to be aware of when taking money from your parents is that you may alienate your siblings if the money is lost. Your siblings may see the lost money as being part of their future inheritance and, therefore, partly as their money. I recall one situation where a father supported the ailing business of his youngest daughter for a number of years and invested several millions of dollars in supporting the business before he passed away. The daughter's siblings were most upset to see that so much of their father's estate had been wasted on propping up a business that ultimately failed as soon as his support was removed. When the daughter's family home was sold up by the bank to recover debts of the business, she could not garner any support from her siblings to assist with keeping the bank at bay.

Professional investors

There is a group of investors who are willing to assume the risks of lending to troubled businesses. These people and organisations are generally professional lenders who will have experience in dealing with distressed businesses and who will understand the risks that they are being asked to accept. Funding provided by these investors will be significantly more expensive than mainstream banks or second-tier lenders. As with mainstream lenders, they will generally seek security over assets as a way of recovering their money if the business fails. You may also expect them to be less forgiving if you default on the terms of the loan agreement.

Some professional investors will be prepared to take an equity interest in your business instead of providing a loan. Some may seek an arrangement that provides a loan but gives them the option of converting all or part of that loan into an equity interest.

The important thing to remember is that a business in trouble represents a high-risk investment, and this class of investor is generally very careful about the level of risk they are prepared to take. They will charge a high price for their funding to compensate them for the high level of risk they are being asked to take. Of course, pricing will vary from investor to investor and from business to business depending on the risk profile of the opportunity.

Equity funding

Another source of funding for businesses is equity funding. Equity funding involves selling off a share in the business to investors, generally by selling shares or trust units. The method of seeking equity investment from third parties can range from a private share offer to family, friends or individuals with whom you are acquainted, to a public offering via a formal fundraising process.

Equity funding is usually resisted by the owners of small and medium sized businesses because it involves foregoing part of their ownership and introduces accountability to other owners of the business.

A business experiencing problems is clearly going to be less attractive to investors or the public at large than a strong, healthy business, so investors will generally seek a high return. Indeed, the returns expected by an equity investor are likely to be significantly higher than the return expected by the provider of debt finance because the equity investor takes a higher level of risk than a debt provider. Some forms of equity or quasi-equity investment (known as "hybrids") have been developed to better manage risk and the cost to the business by blending both debt and equity characteristics.

The advantage of seeking equity funding is that equity does not generally carry a recurrent charge, such as interest, and it is not generally repayable within any specific timeframe. That is not to say that equity funders do not expect a return on their investment. However, the return to an equity investor comes in the form of dividends and capital gains when they sell out of the business. Dividends are only payable out of profits and are generally payable at the discretion of the board based on the capacity of the business to pay the dividends.

Equity funding is, in most jurisdictions, regulated by laws designed to protect small investors from promoters of dodgy investment schemes. Some types of companies and trusts are precluded from offering equity investments. You should check with your lawyer before making any offer of equity in the business. Failure to comply with the relevant laws may be a criminal offence. It may also open the door to future litigation against you by investors if the business fails, on the basis that you took money from investors in breach of the relevant laws.

Offering equity investments to related parties such as directors or existing shareholders is likely to be less heavily regulated than an offer to the public at large, as these parties have a knowledge of, and an existing association with, the business.

PRIVATE SHARE OFFERS

The most common source of funding (debt or equity) for businesses experiencing difficulties is the directors and/or existing shareholders of the business.

Directors of the business will have a very accurate view of the business, the circumstances impacting the business, the opportunities available to turn the business around, and the risks attaching to those opportunities. As such, directors will be able to make an informed decision to invest funds into the business quickly. It is also very common for directors of small to medium businesses to be substantial shareholders in a business. They will, therefore, also benefit from putting in their own money (rather than seeking a third party investment) to preserve their undiluted equity stake in the business and retain control.

Existing shareholders may well include people who are not directors or otherwise actively involved in the management of the business on a day-to-day basis. These shareholders will be less well-informed than directors but are likely to be more willing to invest in the business than third parties. This is partly because they have an understanding of the business and partly because they have an incentive to protect their existing investment by supporting the business.

Another common source of private equity is family and friends who are not existing investors in the business. On most occasions, family and friends will invest on the strength of their relationship with the existing owners/directors and will not conduct thorough due diligence prior to investing. They will see their investment as supporting you rather than as a pure investment. They will, in return, expect you to look after their interests and deliver what you promise.

If you wish to extend your offering beyond your circle of acquaintances by seeking out other individuals who might be willing to invest in your business, you should engage the support of a professional adviser (such as a stockbroker, lawyer or accounting firm) with experience in equity raisings. Stockbrokers and larger accounting firms will usually have a client base of potential investors available. There are likely to be legal obligations requiring that you provide specific information to prospective investors. There can also be civil or criminal penalties for providing false or misleading information, so it would be wise to get legal advice before going down this path. There may be legal restrictions in your jurisdiction on who may be approached with an offer to invest, how many potential investors can be approached, and/or how they may be approached.

PRIVATE EQUITY FUNDS

There are a group of large investment funds that specialise in taking equity positions in businesses. The funds are generally focused on businesses with some scale and significant upside potential. They will usually invest with a five to seven year horizon, and expect to exert a reasonable degree of influence during the term of their investment. This can be a positive for the current owners and directors of the business as these funds can bring strong expertise and experience to bear, as well as deep pockets to support the business. They will expect strong financial disciplines to be applied and a good return on their investment to be available. Most of these funds have minimum investment thresholds of greater than $10 million, so they are generally only an option for sizeable, well-established businesses that are temporarily experiencing issues where there is a clear path to turnaround and to adding value to the business.

BUSINESS ANGELS

There is a specific group of private investors, known as business angels, who specialise in investing equity in small and medium businesses. There are a number of readily accessible business angel websites that serve as conduits between businesses and angels. Most commonly, business angels invest in new, growing businesses, but many will look at businesses in need of working capital support where the business has good growth prospects and sound management.

PUBLIC SHARE OFFERS

Public share offers are offers to issue shares to the public at large where the intention is to list the company on a stock exchange. They require a high level of disclosure and extensive due diligence prior to any funds being raised. They are generally highly regulated and take an extended period of time to bring to fruition. It is usually necessary to have a source of significant interim funding available to meet the pre-listing costs associated with going through the public listing process. Investors in new public offerings are usually sensitive to risk, and a business in trouble represents a high-risk investment.

For these reasons, raising money via a public share offer is unlikely to be a suitable strategy. There may be exceptions where the underlying business is experiencing strong growth, and the problems of the business are a result of lack of working capital; or where the business has valuable intellectual property that could be exploited with additional equity capital. A public fundraising is only likely to succeed where the underlying business is sustainably profitable or has good prospects of becoming profitable and growing. The cost of a public fundraising means that it is not a viable option for small businesses.

It is unusual for the entirety of a business to be sold into a public share offer. The normal practice is for the existing owners to retain a reasonable level of equity in the business. Public share offers are, therefore, most suited to businesses that have significant upside potential that is being frustrated by a lack of equity capital, in circumstances where short-term support can be secured and there is a strong upside message to deliver to potential investors which can be independently verified and supported.

Hybrids

There are financing arrangements that carry the characteristics of both debt and equity. These arrangements are known as "hybrid" funding arrangements (the actual funding documents are called "instruments" and so you will often hear these arrangements referred to as "hybrid funding instruments"). Hybrid funding may be more attractive to specific investors than a pure equity investment or a pure debt investment, as it can offer some of the characteristics of both debt and equity.

The most common hybrid funding instruments are convertible notes and redeemable preference shares.

Convertible notes are essentially interest-bearing loans that may be converted, at the option of the investor ("noteholder") and/or the business, into equity in the business. They can be attractive because they offer investors a regular income (interest) with a future choice to either have their investment returned or converted into a share in ownership of the business (equity) if the business performs well. Where the right to convert the notes to equity rests with the business, it provides the business with the advantage of not having to fund the repayment of the notes if the business is not travelling well when they are due to be either repaid or converted. Clearly, where the business holds the right to convert the investment to equity, the investor carries the risk of being locked into an investment that may depreciate in value.

Redeemable preference shares ("prefs") are a special type of share (equity) in the business that usually enjoy a preferred (but not guaranteed) right to a fixed dividend ahead of ordinary shares, and a priority to repayment of funds subscribed (ahead of ordinary shares) if the business is wound up. The attraction of prefs for investors lies in the priorities they enjoy over ordinary shares. Prefs are conditionally redeemable at a specific time in the future. The advantage for the business of issuing prefs is twofold. First, they entitle the holder to the payment of dividends (which are only payable from profits) rather than interest, so the dividends don't have to be paid if the business isn't profitable; Second they are usually only redeemable at the option of the business, meaning redemption can occur when it best suits the cash flow of the business. Prefs are often referred to as being "cumulative" (meaning any unpaid dividend is accumulated and payable later) or "non-cumulative" (meaning any unpaid dividend is permanently foregone).

There are a variety of permutations of these instruments, and other funding arrangements may also fit into the hybrid category.

Hybrid debt/equity instruments can be legally complex and the terms of the underlying arrangements can sometimes be difficult for the average person to understand. As a minimum, have your lawyer review any financing proposals and advise you of the terms, obligations and legal intricacies of the arrangements so that you clearly understand what you are getting into.

Crowd funding

A recent development in the raising of money for various causes is the advent of crowd funding. While crowd funding is normally limited to supporting needy causes or new opportunities, there is no obvious reason why this source of funds could not be tapped by a business that has problems. Of course, full, open and honest disclosure will be required and there may be limitations or restrictions placed upon the funding request by the crowd funding website. However, if you have a good story to tell and your business has a positive outlook that is constrained only by lack of funds, then you may have a story that will appeal to crowd funders.

Crowd funding usually comes without onerous conditions (often given as a gift) but should be considered as a source of a relatively small amount of money. You should also check any legal obligations that attach to crowd funding

11. Managing your bank in a crisis

This chapter is designed to help you understand how a bank or financier will view your business if it is in trouble, how you can manage the relationship with your bank or financier, and what options and opportunities might be available to secure support or additional funding from your bank or financier. It will also provide you with perspective on your position and help you to identify the important issues you need to address when dealing with your bank, along with some guidelines and ideas on how to develop and present a strategy to your bank that will, hopefully, avoid enforcement action by the bank, even if you are in default.

Working with your bank

Developing an effective strategy to manage your relationship with your bank is one of the most important actions you must take to implement a successful turnaround plan.

For most businesses, a bank is their major source of funding. If your business is in trouble, the chances are that you are experiencing problems with meeting your commitments to your bank. Even if you are meeting all of your commitments to your bank, you may find that you will need support from your bank at some stage via relief from debt payments or an increase in your debt facilities until you can trade out of your difficulties. Either way, you will need to understand how to manage your banking relationship.

If you have bank debt, your bank is one of the major threats to your business. Your bank can also be one of your key allies as you work through your turnaround plan. Which side of the fence your bank falls to will largely be determined by how you manage the relationship with your bank.

Banks are the most powerful of creditors because they will hold direct security over some or all of the assets of your business. In a default situation your bank can take enforcement action. The security that they hold will provide them with the power to take control of the business or other security by appointing an administrator or taking possession of the security. They (either the administrator or the bank itself) will have the power to sell the secured assets to repay your debt to the bank. In many instances the bank will also hold additional security over your personal assets and these, too, may be at risk if the bank takes enforcement action. Your bank may also hold guarantees from other parties such as related businesses, your partner, your parents, friends or business associates, which may also be called up.

On the other hand, your bank is a business itself and banks do not like losing money. They have the capacity to be patient, to provide some relief from onerous loan terms and to provide your business with additional funding if they believe in your plan and in you. Banks will generally try to work with customers who are seeking to do the right thing, provided they consider the position can be salvaged.

In the following sections we will look at some important features of banks and where your business might fit into the mindset of your bank. We will also consider how the bank is likely to manage your business if it is in default of its loan facilities and how you can position yourself to influence how the bank responds to your circumstances.

Be proactive

It is really important that you be proactive in managing your relationship with your bank at the earliest opportunity. Business owners and managers often have insights into their business that lead them to understand that their business is heading into a difficult period well before those insights are available to their bank. The most common response by business managers to these circumstances is to hope that things can be turned around before their bank finds out, based on the (usually) mistaken belief that their bank will either have a diminished view of their business when it comes to future borrowing requests or that their bank may take pre-emptive action against their business before they have had the opportunity to resolve the problem. The difficulty with this approach is that, when their problems are finally exposed to their bank, the bank will probably be surprised or shocked and is often forced to move quickly to protect its position. If it is clear that the problem has been emerging for some time your bank will also be disappointed that you failed to draw the matter to their attention sooner. This may undermine their confidence in your openness and honesty.

If you become aware that your business is heading into a period of difficulty, you should carefully consider bringing your bank in on the position as soon as possible. More often than not, if the bank is given an early warning and appropriate communication is maintained, the bank will assist the business where possible. Importantly, open and honest communication with your bank builds trust, and all good commercial relationships are ultimately founded on trust.

Loan and security arrangements

It is not uncommon for business owners and managers to be unfamiliar with the terms of their bank loans, and especially with the loan default triggers. They will generally know how much they borrowed, how long the money was borrowed for, how much they have to pay each month, and the applicable interest rate. Beyond that, the truth is that most borrowers just sign the mountain of documents put in front of them by their bank and then forget about them. Knowing that the bank's required documentation is there on a "take it or leave it" basis, few borrowers haggle about loan terms or bother to really understand them. This complacency is usually fuelled by the view of the borrower that they will never default on their loan (let's face it – who ever borrows money in the expectation of defaulting?).

So, before we go any further, a brief commentary on typical loans and their structuring might assist your understanding of banks and how they function.

Non-specialised business finance typically takes three forms – come and go cash facilities, term loans and asset finance. Come and go cash facilities, such as overdrafts, are cash facilities where funds are allowed to flow in and out of the facility with an approved facility limit (maximum loan). They generally do not have fixed repayments. Terms loans usually are fully drawn when they are established and then amortise (get repaid) via regular, periodic loan repayments. Some term loans are made available on an interest-only basis, although these are usually made available for a shorter term than amortising loans. Some term loans start out as interest-only and then convert to amortising loans. An amortising loan is referred to as a "principal and interest" or "P&I" loan. Asset finance loans are either leases or hire purchase arrangements. The difference is that an asset being leased is owned by the financier until the lease is paid out (so the financier can depreciate the asset for tax purposes) whereas an asset subject to a hire purchase arrangement is owned by the borrower.

Business loans are usually secured by providing the financier with a charge (encumbrance) over the assets of the business – land and buildings, debtors, stock, cash at bank, and so on. The security taken over land and buildings (which are called "fixed assets" because they do not change) will typically be a mortgage registered on the title of the land. Assets of the business that change as part of the normal course of business (debtors, stock, and cash) are referred to as "floating assets". Security over these assets will normally take the form of a general charge over the assets of the business. Whereas a mortgage will preclude trading in the secured asset without the consent of the financier, a general charge will allow the floating assets to move up and down in the normal course of business without the financier's consent. However, once a financier elects to enforce a general charge, the charge will "fix" against the floating assets held at the time the general charge is enforced.

Business loans are often also secured by guarantees provided by related companies, directors or substantial shareholders. The obligations imposed by these guarantees are often supported (secured) by a mortgage over property owned by the guarantor (the party providing the guarantee). In the case of a small business, the security supporting the guarantee is most commonly a mortgage over the home of the director or major shareholder.

LOAN DEFAULT

There are generally a wide variety of potential defaults under a business loan – covenant breaches, material adverse changes to the business, tax arrears, failure to make required loan payments, personal bankruptcy of a borrower or guarantor, changes to loan securities, and many more. Default in one loan can also be triggered by a default in another loan made to a related party (a borrower, guarantor or even a related business). This type of default is known as "cross default".

Failure to make payments on the loan as required or failure to repay the full amount due to the bank at the time the facility reaches its expiry date, is known as monetary default. This type of default is generally considered as the most threatening to the bank as it is a reliable indicator of financial stress in the customer's business, and an early warning of potential losses for the bank. Monetary default is immediately visible to the bank's systems and is instantly reported. While it is not always directly acted upon, most banks' policies require prompt efforts to restore the loan to order.

Loan default can arise from a number of events and circumstances other than monetary default. Typically, business loans have lending covenants included that will impose obligations upon the borrowing business such as requiring the borrowing business to achieve and maintain specific minimum financial ratios, or requiring the borrower to provide financial reports to the bank within a specific period of time. Breach of a lending covenant is a technical default which will entitle the bank to take enforcement action at its discretion. Changes to loan securities can also trigger a default, although such changes are rare because banks usually register their security so as to limit the capacity of the borrower to deal with the bank's security without their consent. Loan and security documents will also generally include what is known as a "material adverse change" provision that allows the bank to seek to recover its money via enforcement action if, in the reasonable opinion of the bank, there is a material adverse change to the circumstances under which it originally made the loan.

Banks will not generally take enforcement action on the basis of a technical default such as a covenant breach or a material adverse change, unless there are prevailing circumstances that give rise to either serious concerns about the recoverability of its debt or a material dissatisfaction with the customer relationship. You should not, however, ignore the obligations imposed by lending covenants. Nor should you expect that your bank will not take action against your business if you repeatedly breach lending covenants. In rare circumstances, enforcement action by a bank or financier under a technical breach may be a result of events outside of the control of the borrower. I have witnessed circumstances where a lender has relied on a technical default (in the absence of monetary default) to pursue the recovery of monies owed when the bank itself experienced financial difficulties.

An important point to note regarding loan default is that, once you have defaulted, there is usually no obligation upon your bank to waive or forgive that default even if you subsequently make good. The general position is that if you miss a payment or breach covenant periodically your bank will not take any action and it will, by its actions in accepting future payments or compliance with future covenants, be taken to have waived the default. But they are not obliged to do so, and you should not assume that merely making up the missed payments or rectifying a covenant breach will entitle you to return to the position you held prior to the default, particularly once enforcement action by the bank has commenced.

CROSS DEFAULT

Default under any one loan facility of a borrower will usually also give rise to default under all of the other facilities of that borrower.

Default by one borrower can give rise to what is known as cross default, which is where related non-defaulting borrowers are also deemed to be in default of their facilities even if they haven't breached any of their loan conditions. For cross default to occur, the borrowers being cross defaulted need to be related, either by way of guarantees or by way of dependence. Any guarantor of the defaulting borrower's debts may be cross defaulted. Related parties may also usually be caught under provisions of the facility or security documentation. For example, assume company A is a subsidiary of Parentco, and companies B and C are also subsidiaries of Parentco. The loan documentation for loans to companies A, B, C and Parentco would normally provide that if company A defaults on a loan, Parentco, company B, and company C will also be in default of their loans with the bank, even though none of Parentco, company B or company C have breached any of their loan conditions. In most group situations like this, each of Parentco and the subsidiaries would be expected to guarantee each other's loans.

Cross default will also usually extend to the personal debt facilities of any personal guarantors of the debts of the defaulting company (such as directors who have guaranteed the company's debts).

Although cross default is generally an automatic legal effect of a default by one party, it is usually up to the bank to decide if and when it will choose to act upon the cross defaults.

DEFAULT INTEREST RATES

In the first instance, default generally gives rise to the application of default interest rates which are usually quite punitive. Businesses that are in default are often experiencing cash flow difficulties, so default interest rates do not make it any easier to get through periods of cash stress. Periods of extended default interest rates can quickly erode the equity in a business. Moreover, if cross default is applied to other entities within a borrowing group, the impact of default interest rates can be catastrophic.

ENFORCEMENT OF SECURITY

When your business took out a loan from your bank, you would have signed a number of documents including a facility or loan agreement, security documents, and probably a personal guarantee. The security documents give your bank a charge over various securities (assets), and specific rights with respect to those securities, in the event of default under the loan which the assets are securing. The security taken by your bank will comprise a specific charge over some or all of the assets of the business (such as cash, debtors, stock or plant and equipment). Banks usually like to take additional security in the form of mortgages over property where possible, as property is a very strong form of security.

The facility or loan documents will have provided your bank with specific powers in the event of default, including the right to exercise enforcement powers in relation to the securities provided.

Some types of lending are tied to specific classes of assets where the security taken is specifically related to the asset being financed. Examples include asset finance (where a charge over the plant and equipment being financed is taken), factoring/debtor finance (where a specific charge over the debtors of the business is taken), property lending (where a mortgage over the relevant property is taken), and crop funding for farmers (where a crop lien may be taken as security).

The enforcement rights available to your bank will vary depending on the nature of the facilities it has provided to your business and the securities it holds. In most jurisdictions, your bank will be required to serve demands upon a defaulting borrower seeking immediate repayment of the full amount of the outstanding loan prior to commencing any formal enforcement action, although that is not always the case. If the demands for repayment are not complied with, your bank will have the right to take possession of the assets over which it holds security (or appoint someone else to take possession of those assets), and to sell those assets to recoup the outstanding loan and costs associated with recovering and selling the assets. Where the bank has a charge over a business, it may appoint an administrator or receiver and manager to continue to trade the business so that it may sell the business as a going concern.

Enforcement action will also involve terminating credit limits or facilities, calling up guarantees, or suspending or restricting access to your bank accounts. In some cases, these actions will also be applied to the facilities and bank accounts of guarantors. Enforcement action will almost always result in the termination of the banking re-lationship with the customer and, usually, also with any guarantors.

From the bank's perspective, enforcement strategies have the ad-vantage of placing the bank in control of the process of seeking to recover the monies owed. In many jurisdictions there are statutory obligations placed on banks that require the enforcement process to be conducted in a certain manner or under specific rules. When a bank exercises its enforcement rights there is usually a range of costs incurred which can be quite high. These costs might include valua-tion fees, expert advice, marketing expenses, selling agent's com-mission, and professional fees payable to administrators/receivers. All of these costs will be recoverable from the proceeds of the sale of the assets held as security by your bank. The potentially devastat-ing effects of default interest and enforcement costs should provide sufficient incentive for you to act quickly to remedy any default and, where possible, to avoid the application of default interest rates, cross default, and bank driven enforcement action. Banks generally prefer to avoid enforcement action if an acceptable, deliverable, and timely alternative is available.

PERSONAL GUARANTEES

In most cases, particularly where small businesses are concerned, a bank will take personal guarantees from the directors and/or propri-etors of the business, supported by charges over the personal assets of the directors. It is not unusual for the directors/proprietors of a business to pledge their family home as security for business debts.

A common misconception is that banks are required to enforce the security they have over the business assets before they can exercise their rights under personal guarantees. This is not generally correct. Once a loan goes into default it will trigger a right for the bank to call up the full amount of the debt from every guarantor by serv-ing demands under the guarantees. If those demands are not met, the bank may pursue immediate enforcement action against the guarantors and may seek to take possession of, and sell, any property security provided by the guarantor to support their guarantee. This will extend to the personal home of directors if the home has been pledged as security for a personal guarantee. Having said that, most banks will not pursue guarantors until they have realised the direct security provided by the borrower, unless they consider that the guarantor is taking steps to put personal assets out of reach of the bank. In Australia, the Banking Code of Practice enshrines this process. Nevertheless, the threat of enforcement action against the personal assets of directors who have provided personal guarantees is a significant incentive for directors to seek a cooperative solution to the difficulties being encountered by the business.

What matters to banks?

It may sound obvious to say that banks lend money with the intention of getting it back as well as making a return on their investment. When you apply for a loan from your bank, your application is assessed having regard to the capacity of your business to service and repay the loan from its trading activities (the first way out), and also having regard to how the bank might recover its money if the business is unable to service the loan from its trading activities (the second way out). The second way out is generally by way of security over assets of the business such as debtors, trading stock, land and buildings or plant and equipment. The bank will also, in most cases, look to a third way of recovering its money, by taking personal guarantees from the directors of the business. Often these guarantees will be supported by security over property owned by the directors in a personal capacity (such as their homes).

When you borrow money from a bank you enter into a loan agreement in one form or another. You will also undoubtedly be asked to sign documents that provide the bank with the loan security referred to in the preceding paragraph. The loan agreement and security documents will contain conditions – some of which may not seem terribly important at the time you sign up for the loan. For example, one very common provision of security documents is that the bank will have the right to take enforcement action if there is a material adverse change in the financial position of the business or if any other events occur that, in the reasonable opinion of the bank, diminish your capacity to meet your obligations to the bank. The directors of a business are generally very optimistic about its prospects at the time they enter into loan agreements and security documents, so it is rare for loan conditions such as these to be given much thought. In any event, it is unlikely that the bank will allow the loan to proceed if you asked for these provisions to be removed, so there is a general attitude among borrowers of blind acceptance.

Loan agreements always include obligations for customers to make payments of interest, or interest and principal, on a regular basis. Failure to make payments in a timely manner as required by the loan agreement is a monetary default under the loan agreement. It is also common with business loans for covenants to be included in the loan documents. Loan covenants are obligations which require business customers to provide information to the bank and/or apply key financial ratios (working capital ratios are explained in Chapter 1) to the business as default triggers. These ratios might include current ratio, quick ratio, interest times cover ratio, and debt service cover ratio. Material adverse changes to sales, gross profit and net earnings may also be included in loan covenants. Breach of loan covenants is what is known as a technical default under the loan.

It is not unusual for a customer to make a loan payment late for a whole range of reasons. The fact that a payment is late will trigger a report, but it is unlikely to trigger immediate enforcement action – unless there is some prior history that has led the bank to be concerned that a late payment is just the beginning of a very serious problem for the business.

It is also not unusual for business customers to breach loan covenants. A breach of covenant also gives rise to the bank's enforcement rights. However, it is unlikely that a breach of covenant will give rise to enforcement action, except in exceptional circumstances such as when the bank has already established a likelihood that serious problems are, or will be, experienced by the business.

Defaults of any description impact upon the bank's impression of your business as a customer and so they should be avoided if possible. Even if your bank does not take action, it is very common in the case of technical defaults for the bank to advise the customer that, although it may have no intention of taking immediate action, the failure to take action does not waive the default and therefore preserves its rights of enforcement until the default is remedied.

Every bank scores its customers on a risk scale based on their compliance with their obligations to the bank. If you miss payments or fail to meet covenants your risk score will increase. As your risk score increases, so does the mathematical probability that you will ultimately default on your loan. The higher risk of losses means the bank must allocate more of its own money (capital) to the loan. This results in the need for the bank to charge a higher margin to achieve the same return on equity, which will impact on the margin that the bank charges you. Defaults will increase your risk rating and, therefore, impact the interest rate charged on your loans.

All banks have computer systems that closely monitor customer behaviours with respect to account conduct. Both monetary default and technical defaults are monitored. Generally speaking, if monetary defaults persist for more than a few days the bank will take some form of action to have the default remedied. This is because the failure to remedy the default may be an indicator of a more serious underlying problem. Technical defaults, although not generally seen as being as important as monetary defaults, will also be acted upon in most cases if they persist, particularly if the default is one that is indicative of potentially serious deterioration in the capacity of the business to meet its financial obligations to the bank.

The important thing to note is that if you are in default, the bank will be aware of it. They may not take immediate action in the expectation that you will remedy the default, but the existence of the default triggers their enforcement rights and your business is vulnerable as long as the default persists. Moreover, the longer the default exists (particularly with respect to monetary defaults) the more likely it is that the bank will take action to protect its position. You can be certain that if your business is 90 days or more in arrears on one or more of your loans, your business will be flagged for action by your bank.

Some important characteristics of banks

It is worthwhile at this juncture to spend a little time explaining how banks function. Banks are unlike most other commercial businesses and understanding some of their characteristics may help to align your strategies with the expectations of your bank.

Banks are predominantly staffed with people who know nothing but banking as a career. Although many business bankers will hold themselves out as understanding your business, very few bankers have any direct experience of running a business. Their understanding of your business is based on their training and their experience in dealing with a number of businesses in their role as a banker. This gives them a superficial understanding of business. Even fewer bankers will understand what it is to have everything you own under threat. It is important to understand in developing a strategy to manage your banking relationship that the banker you are dealing with will have only a limited understanding of what you are experiencing.

Secondly, banks are large, bureaucratic organisations which have millions of customers and hundreds of millions of accounts. Although they tell you that they provide a personalised service, very few customers receive any form of special attention. You will be referenced in the bank by a customer number. Their size dictates that banks also have very structured policies and procedures. What that means for you as a customer with a business that is in trouble, is that the way in which the bank responds to your circumstances may well be driven at a policy level, so their response may not be a response to your individual circumstances but rather a case of the bank following a defined procedure or policy route. The ability or willingness of the bank to be flexible may well be less than you might expect. Often it will come down to the attitude of the individual banker with whom you are dealing. More on this later.

Thirdly, banks are the most highly indebted (geared) of our large businesses. When a bank lends $1 million to a customer, usually 90% ($900,000) or more of that money has been borrowed by the bank. Only around 10% of the money lent by a bank is the bank's own money. The rest of the money is borrowed from customers (via deposits made with the bank) and institutional lenders, including other banks. The high level of debt means a bank with an equity base of, say, $1 billion can actually lend around $10 billion to its customers. Surprisingly, most banks would consider that level of gearing to be unacceptable if it were to apply to a normal business customer. However, high gearing is the norm for banks.

Banks also operate on tiny margins relative to the scale of their total assets and relative to most other industries. The normal gross interest rate margin for a bank is in the order of 2% to 3%. For a well-run, profitable bank, the annual net profit is likely to be in the order of 1% of total assets. What that means is that a bank with a $1 billion ($1000 million) loan book will have a gross interest rate margin of only $20 $30 million, and a net profit after costs in the order of only

$10 million. That also means that if that same bank loses $1 million (only 0.1% of its total loan book), it will wipe out 10% of its annual profit and it will then need to lend out $100 million (10% of its entire loan book) for a year to recoup that loss.

As these figures demonstrate, banks are very sensitive to losses. The downside of high gearing and thin margins is that banks are very exposed to risk if their loans turn bad. As in the example, our $1 billion bank only has to lose $10 million for its entire profit to be wiped out for a year. Moreover, our bank with $1 billion of assets (loans) only has shareholders' funds of $100 million, so a $10 million loss will wipe out more than 10% of the bank's equity base. Looking at it another way, if a bank loses 10% of the money it has loaned to customers, it will lose all of its equity and will become insolvent.

Of course, most medium to large banks have assets that are measured in the tens of billions or hundreds of billions of dollars, so the numbers required to cause serious problems for a medium to large bank are significantly higher than those for our $1 billion bank. However, on a proportional basis, the numbers are the same. For most banks, loan losses amounting to 1% of their total assets will wipe out a year's profit and materially erode their equity base. Well-managed banks take this risk very seriously.

There are two ways that banks manage the risk of making losses on their loan portfolio. The first is a combination of diversification and scale. The diversification strategy requires that banks manage the level of risk they take in relation to specific asset classes, specific industries and in relation to individual customers. The banks apply what are known as prudential limits to restrict the amount of money they will lend into a specific asset class, industry sector or customer. By doing so they limit the amount of potential losses they can incur if any particular asset class, industry or customer experiences a severe downturn or collapses. The scale component of risk management involves spreading the risk over a very large customer base.

The second strategy adopted by banks to manage their downside risk is a range of internal policies and procedures that are designed to identify and manage situations where a loss risk may emerge. The exact process adopted varies from bank to bank but, generally speaking, most banks have computer systems that provide them with an early warning of deterioration in the financial position of their customers. As noted earlier, these systems track compliance with loan obligations and assign a progressive risk score to each customer. Most business customers of banks will have experience with the use of lending covenants by their bank. Lending covenants usually apply a combination of reporting obligations to keep the bank informed of the customer's financial position, and may also require financial performance ratios to be calculated. It is by keeping itself abreast of the financial position of the customer that the bank is able to detect any change or adverse trend in the financial soundness of the business. Lending covenants form an important part of a bank's early warning system.

Banks will also regularly review specific industries that might be of concern or where there might be an expectation of future stress. Loans to the agricultural sector might be reviewed after a major storm season or a long drought. Export industries and customers whose businesses are focused on export sales might be reviewed if there is a substantial upturn in the local currency. Mining businesses might be reviewed when a downturn in commodity prices becomes evident. Most banks employ a team of economists to provide advice on the future outlook on a macro-economic level. The industry in which your business operates will also be given a risk rating, and that rating will impact on the overall credit assessment for your business.

Following the massive damage to the banking industry arising from the GFC, the amount of capital held by banks to underwrite loan losses and the manner in which they manage the risks to which their business is exposed are both closely monitored by regulatory authorities in each country. Prior to the GFC most banks operated with capital ratios well below 10% (less than 10% of their lending was covered by the bank's own money). Post GFC, most banks have been required to increase their capital to make them more resilient to economic downturns.

Banks also usually require their frontline business bankers to maintain an understanding of, and to periodically visit, the customer's business. These visits are more than just a friendly interaction designed to build a rapport with the customer. They are an opportunity for the banker to observe the customer's business in action. An experienced banker will notice significant changes to stock levels and other indicators of business activity that might provide a hint that things are not going well. An experienced banker will also ask questions designed to gain a clear understanding of the current and likely future trading position of the business.

How banks usually deal with a business that is in trouble

A useful starting point in developing a strategy to manage your banking relationship is to understand the way banks deal with business customers that are experiencing problems.

Your bank will have millions of business customers and, over the years, thousands of those businesses will have experienced periods of difficulty. Banks understand that businesses get into trouble and they have many years' experience in dealing with customers whose businesses are in distress. They have a very good understanding of what causes business failure. Indeed, one might reasonably expect that, with all these years of experience, banks might have learned how to avoid businesses that will fail. Unfortunately for banks, that is not the case.

As discussed, banks monitor the compliance with the terms of their loans. Most of this monitoring is electronic, making the detection of some adverse behaviours instantaneous. Failure to make scheduled payments on time is easily and closely monitored. Banks also identify adverse changes in the financial performance of businesses by failure to meet loan covenants. Periodic review of the financial reports of a business, and applying financial ratios, allows the bank to monitor financial trends that may impact upon the ability of the business to meet its obligations to the bank. Adverse trends such as deteriorating profitability and/or losses, a weakening balance sheet, tax arrears, and breach of the key financial ratios also provide banks with an insight into the changing risk profile of the customer.

Once deterioration in a customer's financial position is identified, the bank will usually review all available information to assess whether or not the deterioration represents an imminent threat to the capacity of the customer to meet its obligations to the bank. If the review evidences the likelihood that the customer will be unable to meet all of its obligations to the bank in a timely manner, the bank will implement a process to monitor the customer and manage the downside risk represented by the deterioration in the customer's position. If the risk is assessed as modest or temporary or otherwise not serious, it is likely that the bank will simply monitor the trading performance of the business more closely than it has in the past. However, if the risk is assessed as material, the bank will take more positive steps to protect its position. Most banks have specialist teams to manage business customers who are experiencing difficulties where the bank assesses that there is a material risk the customer will not be able to meet its obligations to the bank. These teams go by various names which are generally linked to asset management, specialised business services or specialised lending services.

HOW WILL I KNOW IF MY FILE IS UNDER THE MANAGEMENT OF A SPECIALIST TEAM?

Your bank may not necessarily tell you that the management of your file has been changed to a specialist risk management team. If your business is experiencing cash stress, is making losses or has defaulted on loan obligations (whether that be by failure to meet lending covenants or by missing loan payments) and you suddenly find yourself with a new bank manager, you can probably assume that your business is now in the hands of a specialist risk management team within the bank, particularly if your new manager is located in head office rather than your local branch. However, in many instances you will continue to deal with the same bank manager and the specialist team will be working in the background making decisions about how the bank should respond to your position. Generally, the specialist team will be charged with developing a strategy to manage the downside risk to the bank (the risk of the bank incurring losses), and the specialist unit will become the decision-making authority on your file. Even if the bank doesn't tell you that your file has been transferred to a specialist team there will probably be some indications that things have changed. Your regular bank manager may tell you that he has to refer matters to head office for a decision, you may find relatively minor requests for funding increases declined, or your regular manager may simply start asking for more and more information in an atypical manner. Most banks will not lie to you about the transfer of your file to a specialist team; they simply may not be proactive in telling you that the change has occurred. So, do not be afraid to ask the question if you suspect that there has been a change in the management of your file.

WHAT SHOULD I DO IF I FIND THAT MY FILE IS BEING MANAGED BY A SPECIALIST TEAM?

Transfer of your file to a specialist risk management team is not necessarily a bad thing as these teams are usually staffed with people who are used to dealing with businesses that are experiencing difficulties and who understand the options available to manage and resolve problems in business. They are often also given wider authority than is generally available within the bank to allow for flexibility and speed in the development of strategies to resolve risks to the bank's position. On the other hand, the experience of the specialist risk management team means that they are likely to be very astute and unlikely to accept a wait-and-see attitude on the part of the customer. They are generally charged with the obligation of developing proactive strategies to manage the bank's risk and they will want to see a clear path to the resolution of the issues of concern.

It is likely that the management of your file will be delegated to a single manager within the specialist team, although smaller customers (with, say, less than $1 million of business debt) may end up in a specialist team who are required to follow specific policies in the collection of the bank's debts. The larger the bank's exposure to your business the more likely it is that a single, experienced manager will have responsibility for the file. The size and nature of the exposure that will lead the management of your file higher up the totem pole within the specialist team will vary from bank to bank. If possible, you should try to develop a direct line of contact with the person (or people) within the specialist team who is/are managing your file. Often this will not be possible, but if it is possible take advantage of the opportunity to try to develop a rapport with your file manager within the specialist team. That person (or those people if there is more than one manager involved in controlling your file) will be the one who you will need to convince of the benefit of helping you through the difficult times your business is experiencing. They are the people who will determine if your turnaround strategy is acceptable to the bank. They are the team who will make the decision to appoint an insolvency practitioner to the business or take possession of securities if they are not convinced there is a workable strategy to remedy the issues being experienced by the business.

It is often the case that the file manager within the specialist team will have sole authority and you will be subject to their interpretation of the situation and their view as to the most appropriate strategies to manage the bank's risk. As such, even though banks have policies around the management of defaulting customers, individual personalities can come into play, as can the personal attitudes and leanings of your manager. It is unlikely that you will be able to change these attitudes or leanings, but it could be a significant advantage to understand them. For example, your manager may not favour providing any increased funding to your business to help it out of its difficulties (which would increase the potential losses to the bank if the strategy failed) but instead may prefer a "cut and run" strategy to reduce the loss risk to the bank. Also, developing a rapport with your manager in the specialist area personalises the relationship and potentially improves the chances of receiving their support. Of course, personalising the relationship can work against you if you antagonise or upset the manager you are dealing with, and you need to decide whether or not you are able or willing to seek a positive relationship with the specialist team before you start trying to develop direct contact with your manager within the specialist team.

If you cannot make direct contact with the specialist manager, then seek to maintain a strong relationship with your existing manager. They will be the conduit between you and the decision makers and your relationship with them will impact upon the level of support they provide for your turnaround plan.

What does your bank think of your business?

Most banks go to great lengths to convince their customers that they care about the customer at an individual level. While that is a genuine objective of the banks, managing millions of customers requires a broad-brush approach to customer management. Consider our $1 billion bank. If every single customer in that bank had a $1 million loan there would be 1000 customers. You, as a single customer who owed $1 million to the bank, would represent 1/1000 of the bank's customer base and lending book. You would represent a very small part of the customer base. Now, think about the fact that most banks have lending books that are measured in the hundreds of billions of dollars, and in some cases in the trillions of dollars, and most customers have loans well under $1 million, and you will realise that most banks have millions of customers. Despite the efforts of banks to make you feel important in their marketing, in the overall scheme of things you are unlikely to be more than a tiny blip on the radar. Customers often fail to understand just how insignificant they are in the overall scheme of things.

Your importance to the bank increases once you are in default of your facilities because you will then represent a risk of losses. That is not to say that you will become a favoured customer. Rather, you will be attracting attention from your bank for the wrong reasons.

In most cases, although you may receive correspondence or a call from your local manager, the bank probably won't get too serious until you reach some internally-defined trigger point. That trigger is often, but not always, being overdue for 90 days or more. Up to that point in time you have the opportunity to either remedy the default or develop a plan to resolve the difficulties being experienced by your business. That is not to say that the bank will not pay attention to you or that you can slip under their radar. Don't assume that because you haven't heard from the bank that they haven't noticed that you are in default, as defaults are invariably monitored electronically these days. In some cases, they won't tell you what they are doing until it is too late for you to do anything about it.

The size of your business debt will impact how your business fits into the bank's defaulting customer mindset. Generally speaking, the smaller the debt the more routine the collection procedures adopted by the bank will be. At the bottom end of loan size, it is probably not much more than a numbers game for the bank and they will apply a "sausage machine" process in most instances. On the other hand, smaller business borrowers are generally better protected by legislation or regulation that will limit or direct the enforcement option available to the bank. Just what defines a small business loan will vary from bank to bank. Anything under $1 million is likely to be considered small by most banks.

Even so, banks are very vulnerable to losses and very focused on loss risk management. It is in the interests of the bank to try to minimise their loss risk. That means that, if you are able to align your objectives with the objectives of the bank, it is possible to secure their support. If your business has long-term upside potential, all the better, because turning your business around can provide the bank with a loyal, long-term customer. However, if your account is managed by a specialist manager, their primary objective will be to minimise and hopefully eliminate the risk of losses to the bank. Turning around a business for the purpose of establishing a long-term business relationship will be a secondary consideration if your business is in default. Again, the propensity of the bank to favour a turnaround strategy as opposed to an exit strategy will be influenced by the individual attitudes of the manager who is looking after your file.

Developing a strategy to deal with your bank

Before you commence negotiations with your bank, you should have a clear idea in your mind where you wish to go with the negotiations and what role you hope the bank will play in your plans.

You should have identified a strategic framework within which you want the ultimate outcome of the negotiations with the bank to fall and, in doing so, you should have defined the outcomes you believe both you and the bank will be able to live with. It is unlikely that you will be able to specify exactly what the bank will do in all respects, so a range of acceptable outcomes is probably a more suitable strategy than limiting yourself to a specific set of requirements. For example, you may determine that, as a minimum, you must secure at least three months' relief from loan payments for your business to survive but that your business would be in a much more comfortable position if you were able to secure six months' relief from loan payments.

Dealing with your bank when your business is in default of its loan conditions can be an intimidating process. The bank usually holds a stronger negotiating position because of its rights to take enforcement action against your business if your business is in default. It is usually the case that business owners will have guaranteed the debts of their business and secured that guarantee by a charge over their personal assets (such as the family home). Many business owners and managers will find themselves both uncertain as to what they can or should do to remedy their position, and fearful that their bank will take punitive action that will deprive them of much of their life's work and everything they own.

Nevertheless, developing a strategy to deal with your bank is likely to be critical to the survival of your business. The strategy you develop to deal with your bank should be an integral part of your strategy to turn around or save your business.

When you are framing your strategy, incorporate an understanding of the following into your thinking:

- Unless you owe the bank an amount measured in the tens of millions, you are unlikely to be much more than a number, so your negotiation starts from a weak position (even weaker if you are in default).

- It is not unusual to experience serious emotional stress when your business is under pressure. Try not to bring that emotional stress to the negotiating table with your bank.

- Do not be belligerent or aggressive unless you consider there is a clear strategic advantage in doing so. There will be circumstances where a strong approach will be advantageous but this will not generally be the case. You will usually get much further if you are calm, rational, and polite.

- Remember, you are one of many who have been down this path with the bank and there is unlikely to be anything particularly new in what you have to deliver. Your bank will have seen it all before.

- Your bank will have policies and procedures to address business customers who are in default. Those procedures will probably involve your file being managed by a specialist unit once you pass the trigger point for active involvement by the bank in managing the risks presented by your defaulting business. The manager dealing with your file in a specialist unit will probably have significant power to make decisions that may impact upon your business. Winning the support of that manager for your strategies and proposals may be the key to securing the support of your bank.

Consider using an adviser

In negotiations with your bank the stakes are high, and if you are not totally comfortable in your understanding of the playing field or the rules of the game, you should consider appointing an expert adviser to assist you with developing your strategy. It is unlikely that you will have had any experience in dealing with your bank when your business has been in default. You should not feel inadequate because you are uncertain in these circumstances. It is unfamiliar territory and you will be navigating your business through some potentially treacherous waters. A good adviser will help you to understand the expectations and requirements of your bank, clearly identify the significant issues to be resolved with your bank, assist you to understand the key financial issues that will be of interest to your bank, help you to prepare accurate forecasts, and help you to quantify your financial needs to the bank. You may also require legal advice to assist your understanding of your legal rights and obligations and the legal framework within which the bank operates.

Good advisers don't usually come cheap and businesses in trouble are usually strapped for cash, so managers often resist appointing advisers due to the high cost. However, if money is a big concern, try negotiating an arrangement whereby your adviser receives a substantial incentive for a successful outcome and a lesser sum if the outcome is unsuccessful. Some advisers may even be prepared to work on a success-fee-only basis. An experienced adviser can be an asset who can bring an understanding of the expectations of the bank and assist in building a strategy that is acceptable to the bank. Be cautious in selecting your adviser. Some advisers will try to sell themselves to you as being experienced in assisting businesses through difficult times and, therefore, qualified to advise you. Most of these people will not be experienced enough in the workout/banking space to provide you with the best possible advice. Look for an adviser who can specifically demonstrate experience in negotiating settlements with customers of a similar scale and, preferably, with the same bank. Ask for references from business owners and managers who have been helped by your prospective adviser.

Understand your financing needs

There is no point in approaching your bank for support or assistance if you don't know the nature and extent of the support and assistance your business requires. Understanding the needs of your business is a fundamental component of any turnaround or work-out plan. In the context of dealing with your bank, your ability to define and articulate your needs will not only facilitate a clear understanding by the bank but will also demonstrate to your bank that you understand your business and its circumstances, and that you have thought about your requirements.

Cash flow problems are a universal issue for businesses that are in trouble, so it is highly likely that your most significant need will be assistance in managing your cash flow. There are various ways in which your bank may be able to help you to manage through a period of tight cash flow. These options are discussed next.

What can you ask for from your bank?

Although your bank will undoubtedly have its own views on what level of support it is willing to provide to your business, you should have a clear idea of what support you will be seeking from your bank.

The support and assistance your bank is willing and able to provide to your business will vary from bank to bank but will generally comprise one or more of the following:

- a short-term excess (an increase in debt funding for a period of a few days or weeks)
- a permanent increase in debt facilities
- capitalisation of interest charges for a period of time (where interest is added to the debt instead of having to be paid)
- suspension or deferral of loan repayments for a period of time
- suspension or deferral of the principal component of loan repayments for a period of time (reverting the loan to interest-only so only interest is payable and the debt does not reduce)
- extension of the term of the loan to reduce the amount of regular payments

- refinancing of a residual on a lease or hire purchase agreement
- a temporary or permanent reduction in interest rates
- a change in the timing of loan repayments to reflect seasonal business cash flows
- change to a more flexible or cheaper loan product
- guarantees to suppliers
- a change in loan securities
- a release of specific loan securities without debt reduction
- relief for a period of time from (future) interest charges
- a discount on your debt (debt forgiveness).

The last of these options is likely to be the least palatable to your bank as it will result in the bank making a loss. The third last option (release of specific loan securities) is also likely to be frowned upon by your bank, as it increases the risk of losses unless the consideration provided for the release of the security is at least equal to what the bank believes the security would realise if it was sold (net of costs) or the bank is very strongly secured. All of the other options may, alone or in concert with other options, provide the bank with the opportunity to recover all of its debt by assisting your business to transition through the difficult times.

Your bank is not a charity

The most important thing to understand and to keep in your mind at all times, is that your bank is not a charity. Your bank is a business just like your business in that it exists to make profits for its shareholders. Many business customers who experience problems and default on their facilities believe that they are owed some form of forbearance or relief by their bank. They believe that their years of being dedicated customers entitles them to some form of preferential treatment, whether or not the preferential treatment expected makes commercial sense. You should not expect your bank to carry you through difficult times just because you feel you deserve it.

Treat your negotiations with your bank as a business dealing. Banks are businesses and they will act commercially in most instances. Any proposal you put to your bank will therefore need to pass the test of commercial reality. You will need to be able to demonstrate to your bank that your proposal is deliverable and that it will result in an outcome for the bank that is (preferably) better than the outcome any alternative strategy would deliver. A better outcome for the bank is generally (and most easily) measured in terms of the total financial return to the bank.

Not all decisions taken by your bank will be driven purely by financial considerations and, in some cases, it may also be possible to demonstrate other reasons why a strategy should be pursued even though it results in a potentially worse outcome for the bank than taking enforcement action. Decisions that make commercial sense for a bank may include consideration of factors such as potential damage to the reputation of the bank, the risk of setting a precedent that other customers may seek to exploit, the cost and diversion of resources to litigation, and political issues (such as whether an action may have regulatory consequences). The reputation of the bank can be impacted by adverse publicity, adverse social media coverage, customer complaints, and word-of-mouth discussion of customer problems.

These days, many banks are also demonstrating that they have a social conscience (possibly even that they have a heart) and are willing to compromise their position where there are strong compassionate grounds. Where hardship caused by unforeseen circumstances such as serious ill-health, loss of employment or natural disasters has resulted in an inability on the part of the customer to meet loan repayments, banks are often willing to agree to arrangements to assist customers through these difficult times. In some jurisdictions there are formal regulations or voluntary industry standards that require banks to consider providing relief where exceptional circumstances result in customer hardship.

Mutual trust is essential

As with any business transaction, both sides have to expect that the other side is acting in good faith towards a mutually acceptable solution. You cannot expect your bank to act commercially and in good faith if you are not reciprocating the good faith (or when your bank believes you are not acting in good faith). Your bank may consider factors such as failure to disclose material facts, lying to them, or seeking to alienate assets or securities to protect them from action by the bank as acts of bad faith. In some cases, your bank may also consider efforts to refinance to another financial institution as an act of bad faith (although if the bank has concerns about the future viability of your business or the risk of making losses on your facilities, it may actually encourage and support efforts to refinance).

In most cases transparent, open, and honest communication with your bank will be a vital part of securing their trust and, ultimately, their support.

Time is risk to a bank

The longer any strategy takes to implement the greater the likelihood that unforeseen events will intervene and impact upon the outcome being sought. Time also impacts upon the ability of the bank to reinvest the funds recovered to start earning a return via new lending. Accordingly, in framing any proposal to be put to your bank, you should have regard to the time it will take to reach the target outcome. All other things being equal, two strategies that deliver comparable financial outcomes will be measured against the time taken to achieve the desired outcome, with the shorter timeframe being favoured.

Your bank is a secured creditor

Remember that your bank is, in the vast majority of cases, a secured creditor. As such, if you are asking for more money the bank will want to know what additional security you might be willing to provide to support that additional debt. The fact that you do not have any additional security to offer does not preclude you from asking for additional support from your bank, but it will make it more difficult to secure approval from the bank.

As a secured creditor, your bank will hold security over the assets of your business and, often, over your personal assets. The bank will have first priority to receive the proceeds of the sale of these assets ahead of unsecured creditors such as suppliers, tax authorities, and employees, although in some jurisdictions tax authorities and employees enjoy statutory priority to some extent over secured lenders.

What should you ask for from your bank?

To answer this question, take the time to stand back and consider what options are available to your bank and what outcomes each of those options might deliver to your bank. With respect to each strategy that you identify, consider not only the likely financial returns (to the bank) but also the risks (to the bank) associated with the relevant strategy, and the amount of time it will take to implement and complete each strategy. When a business is in trouble there are usually only two or three strategy options available. These can usually be divided into cooperative strategies and enforcement strategies. Your objective should be to get your bank to agree to a cooperative strategy. Enforcement strategies generally arise when a bank is unable to reach agreement on a cooperative strategy, where there is no cooperative strategy offered or where the bank considers that a materially better or faster outcome can be achieved through enforcement.

COOPERATIVE STRATEGIES

As the name implies, cooperative strategies involve the customer and the bank working cooperatively to undertake an agreed set of actions directed at achieving a mutually understood outcome. For example, the bank may provide some short-term additional funding support to assist the business through a difficult period, with the expectation that the additional funding will be repaid within a predetermined period of time and the business will, thereafter, be able to function normally within existing debt limits. Alternatively, a cooperative strategy might involve the voluntary sale of assets by the customer to reduce debt rather than a forced sale of those assets by the bank. This strategy might be adopted with the expectation that a voluntary sale will achieve a higher price than a sale where the market perceives a forced sale. From the customer's perspective, a voluntary sale has the advantages of not exposing their financial distress to the world, allowing them to have an active role in the sale of the assets, and the prospect of potentially achieving a higher price. Cooperative strategies can also be advantageous for the bank. They are non-confrontational, usually require less management effort on the part of the bank, avoid the risk of legal action by disgruntled customers, generally offer returns that are better than those that would be achieved via enforcement strategies, and offer the prospect of retaining a customer. A successful cooperative strategy can not only result in an ongoing business relationship with the customer but it can, in fact, actually lead to a stronger relationship due to the mutual respect and trust that is developed during the process.

Understandably, customers frame their preferred strategies with their own objectives in mind and almost always prefer to retain control. Cooperative strategies can often be designed to align both bank and customer objectives while the customer retains control of the process. However, cooperative strategies often come undone where there is a difference between the expectations of the customer and the expectations of the bank. The most common of these differences can be found in asset values where the customer, having worked hard to acquire or build an asset, has developed an emotional attachment to the asset and is reluctant to sell it for less than he or she considers to be fair value. Often, the customer's view of "fair value" is more directly related to either the cost of the asset or the amount of debt they need to clear than it is to the current market value of the asset. Banks, on the other hand, will have no emotional attachment to the asset and will be more interested in a timely sale than the highest possible price. This difference in price expectations can lead to customers missing or rejecting sale opportunities in favour of seeking a better price that more closely aligns with their view of fair value. This can result in the bank losing confidence in the customer's willingness to "meet the market" and the bank assuming control of the sale process. An up-front agreement on a minimum acceptable price for an asset being sold is a useful way of avoiding this sort of dispute.

Another example of the differences in expectations that can arise is where the customer believes assets should be sold in a certain order, which generally reflects a hope that the sale of less desirable assets will clear the debt and allow them to retain their preferred assets. This can lead to more saleable assets being held back from the market while less saleable assets flounder in the market.

Selling your strategy to your bank

When seeking to garner your bank's support for a cooperative strategy, consider carefully how your plan is going to look to your bank. Try to remove all your personal prejudices and bias from this analysis and to assess your strategy in the context of the bank's objectives.

It seems obvious to say that the less you ask for, the more likely you are to receive what you have requested from your bank, so the tendency is generally to ask for the minimum level of support that may be required. This is a valid position to take if you are very comfortable that you can fully deliver upon your proposal within the target timeframe. If, for example, you have an unconditional contract of sale on a security property with a definite settlement date that will provide sufficient funds to fully clear your debt, then you can probably be confident in saying to your bank that you will be able to pay out your debt by a specific date. However, it is my experience, and no doubt the experience of most business managers, that things never work out exactly as planned. There are numerous external factors beyond the control of managers that can impact upon a business in a relatively short period of time and these contingencies are often ignored in the development of workout strategies.

Your bank will expect you to understand your business better than they do and they will expect you to be aware of the possible contingencies that may impact upon your business (albeit that no-one can actually predict all external contingencies). If your bank agrees to accept your strategy and provide the required support, and you then fail to deliver upon that strategy, your credibility will be diminished. If, at that time, you seek further forbearance or support from the bank, the bank will be more reluctant to provide further support. The failure of your first attempt will have undermined its confidence in your ability to forecast the performance of your business and/or deliver expected outcomes.

As a starting point for negotiations with your bank, you should seek a level of support (financial support, relief from debt obligations, and timing), that incorporates a reasonable level of contingency to the point where you have a high degree of comfort that you will be able to deliver the stated outcomes within the expected timeframe. It is much better to exceed expectations than to fall short. Your bank will understand the need for contingencies in your forecasting, although they may place conditions around the additional support necessarily arising from the contingencies.

Most banks have flexible policies that will result in the bank being supportive of reasonable requests that involve forbearance, rather than debt forgiveness. Forbearance includes deferring, reducing, extending or otherwise varying loan repayments to assist your business to meet its obligations through the period of difficulty.

Increased debt funding is more problematic. There is an old saying in banking that goes "your first loss is your best loss", meaning that it is often considered unwise to lend out more money in the hope of increasing the bank's ultimate recovery from a troubled business. Many bankers consider this to be sending good money after bad. Requests for additional funding from a defaulting customer will be carefully and thoroughly scrutinised and increased funding will be more difficult to secure than forbearance. Asking for more money is asking the bank to take on a higher exposure to your business at a time when your business is having problems. As such, you will be asking the bank to take on a higher level of risk and to increase the level of potential losses it may incur. Increased funding can be secured if there is a strong, sustainable business case, and where capacity to service and repay the increased debt can be demonstrated.

Increased funding will be easier to obtain where the bank is well secured. If your bank considers that the additional funding risk is well covered by the security it holds then the incremental risk you are asking the bank to take will be mitigated. Provided that you are able to demonstrate how the business will service and repay the additional funding, the request is likely to receive a favourable hearing.

Many businesses experience cash flow problems as a result of poor working capital management. Your bank is unlikely to support a request for additional funding where better management of your stock, debtors and creditors would provide the additional funding required by the business. Your bank will also be reluctant to provide additional funding to pay unsecured creditors, bearing in mind that these creditors rank behind the bank if the business fails.

In limited circumstances, for example where there is no other obvious source of funding for these purposes, your bank may be willing to provide additional funding that is demonstrably necessary to realise an asset or generate funds that will be used to reduce your bank debt or clear arrears. Where realisation costs must be incurred, the bank may prefer to take enforcement action and incur the expenditure in realising a security so they control the process.

It is better to ask your bank to defer $100,000 of loan repayments than it is to ask your bank to give you another $100,000 so that you can meet those loan repayments. If you do ask for additional funding, make sure you clearly demonstrate how that funding will improve your position and how and when the additional funding will be repaid to the bank.

It is unlikely that you will succeed with a request for debt forgiveness. Debt forgiveness involves the bank permanently reducing the debt to an amount that the customer can afford to repay. Writing off part of a customer's debt as part of a workout strategy will generally only be acceptable where the alternative is a substantially larger loss, a very protracted debt recovery process, litigation or material reputational risk to the bank.

A request from your business to release security is also unlikely to get a favourable hearing unless, upon releasing the security, the bank receives an amount equal to at least the net proceeds that might be expected to be recovered from the security if it were realised.

Know your banker

At any point in time hundreds of your bank's business customers will be experiencing some degree of distress. It is also highly likely that your bank will have dealt in the past with customers experiencing similar difficulties to those being experienced by your business. As such, they will understand the circumstances and will probably have had experience in testing out different strategy options to resolve similar difficulties to those you are experiencing. This is particularly true if you are dealing with the specialist unit. The bank's previous experience with similar situations may work in your favour, or may work against you, depending on the bank's prior experience and their attitude.

In developing a strategy to submit to the bank you should consider two things:

1. Due to the sheer number of defaulting customers being managed you may find it difficult to get a decent hearing. As a general rule, the smaller your business debt the more difficult it will be for you to secure the opportunity to implement a unique proposal.

2. Your bank may not move quickly to respond to your circumstances. The best way to differentiate your business from other businesses in the same circumstances is to seek to establish a rapport with your manager (if possible, with the manager in the specialist unit) and to develop a relationship of trust with the bank. The individual managing your file is a human being and subject to the frailties and sensitivities of human beings. None but the most ruthless of managers like to see customers endure the stresses of a collapsing business, lose their businesses, and/or lose their homes. That said, many people who work within the specialist units see so many businesses in trouble that they often become somewhat immune to it. Usually they are obliged to seek to maximise the bank's return which means, of necessity, that they are obliged to pursue all securities available to the bank in their efforts to recover the bank's debt.

Nevertheless, you should start with the view that your manager is a genuine person who will give you a fair hearing and who, while seeking the best commercial outcome for the bank, will also be interested in finding a solution that minimises the damage and angst caused to customers. The exception to this rule will be customers who have established themselves as uncooperative, aggressive, and/or litigious. Typically, the more grief you seek to impose on the bank the more forceful you may expect the bank's response to be. I will talk more on this point later. Until you learn otherwise, start with an open mind in terms of your bank's attitude toward you and believe that they have your interests at heart (albeit that your interests may be secondary to their own interests).

Establishing a rapport with your manager and building trust with the bank will require communication on a regular basis. It will require an open and honest approach with full disclosure and recognition that, whatever solution is found, the bank's interests and rights must be taken into account. Most people will be able to establish fairly quickly whether or not they are being successful in their efforts to establish a rapport with their manager. If you feel you are not getting a fair hearing from your manager, you might consider escalating your concerns to a higher authority within the bank.

If your facilities are already in default and you have a good relationship with your banker, they may be willing to provide you with written advice as to their intended course of action and their expectations.

Understand your legal position

Your ability to negotiate a satisfactory arrangement with your bank will predominantly hinge on your ability to define the needs of your business and demonstrate the commercial merit, and the benefit to your bank, of whatever forbearance or additional support you may be seeking.

Before you begin negotiating with your bank it will pay to ensure that you understand the legal position you are in and the legal position of the other borrowers and guarantors to the debt facilities of the business. It will also be of benefit to you if you understand the legal, moral and ethical framework within which the bank operates.

Understanding your own legal position will ensure that your strategy addresses all of your facilities and securities, and all of the rights and obligations that flow to the business and to you personally from the facility terms and security documentation. You should also understand the legal position of others who may be impacted by enforcement action arising from any default under your debt facilities. These potentially impacted parties may include other related businesses or corporations, co-borrowers, and guarantors.

An understanding of the legal position should also include an understanding of the rights and obligations that flow to your bank from the facility and security documentation. This will allow you to understand what action the bank is entitled to take, the processes that the bank may have to follow, the timeframes that may apply, and the consequences of the bank's actions. This will enable you to ensure your strategy removes (or at least significantly reduces) the risk of the bank taking action against you or others that you did not expect or contemplate, while your strategy is being implemented. Understanding your legal position and the legal position of any other borrowers or guarantors should be a precursor to any negotiations with your bank.

As mentioned previously, when you took out your loans from the bank you will have signed legal documentation in the form of one or more facility agreements and security documents. The security documents will have included one or more of the following:

- property mortgages
- a charge or charges over assets of the business

- personal guarantees and indemnities
- undertakings (which are promises to do certain things at certain times in the future), warranties (whereby you certify that information provided to the bank is correct and complete), and possibly negative pledges (which are promises not to do something such as borrowing from other lenders without the bank's consent).

These legal documents will have conveyed a raft of rights and obligations, with the rights predominantly likely to be in favour of the bank and the obligations predominantly applicable to the borrowers or guarantors.

Most borrowers and/or guarantors generally pay little attention to the detail of the contractual arrangements they enter into with their bank at the time of taking out a loan. Having access to the funds you are seeking provides the opportunity to pursue whatever expenditure you had in mind for the funds and this is exciting, far more exciting than worrying about what might happen if things turn sour. Borrowers do not take out loans with the expectation that their business will fail. Moreover, the legal documents are generally too copious and complex for most people to understand and absorb. Even those people who take the time to seek independent legal advice often fail to understand, or have regard to, the possible consequences of default. It is only when the business faces the prospect, or reality, of the bank enforcing its rights under the facility documents and/or the security documents that borrowers and guarantors focus on the detail of the agreements.

Don't beat yourself up if you didn't take the time to understand the consequences of default when you took out the loan. Very few people do, and very few laypersons are equipped to understand the complexities of the legal documentation attaching to debt facilities and securities. Banks, on the other hand, are very experienced at dealing with legal issues surrounding their documentation so they have a very good understanding of their legal rights and obligations. This places borrowers and guarantors at a disadvantage unless they have sound independent legal advice. So now that your business is experiencing some difficulties, if you don't have a clear understanding of the legal position you are in, you should talk to a good lawyer who is experienced in dealing with banks.

Providing legal advice is beyond the scope of this book; however, there are several important legal issues listed here that will apply in most cases and that need to be understood early on:

- It is common for the facilities of related companies to be linked in the default provisions of the loan documentation. Facility documentation will usually provide that default by one borrower will trigger an automatic default under other related facilities. As outlined previously, this is referred to as cross default. The related facilities will include other loans in the name of the same borrower, loans where there are joint borrowers (one of whom is the defaulting borrower), and loans made to the parties who have guaranteed the debts of the defaulting borrower. Cross default can apply even if the cross defaulted facilities have been operated entirely within the terms of their contractual agreement with the bank. As a practical matter, banks will generally limit the extent to which they apply the cross-default provisions of their documentation. Nevertheless, you should be aware of the existence of cross defaults as they are often used by the banks as either a negotiating tool or a mechanism to recover their debt via access to alternative securities.
- You should not assume that the bank will act to recover its debts from the assets of the business before it turns to the personal guarantees of the directors or other securities that it may hold. The bank can generally act to recover its debt under any of its securities in any order, and each separate recovery action

can be for the full amount of the debt once a loan is in default. That means that, if the bank wishes to do so, personal guarantees can be called upon for the full amount of the outstanding debt before the assets of the business are sold. The bank may also sell any of the property securities it holds in any order. The bank can be taking action under multiple securities at any time until it recovers its full debt. No borrower, guarantor or security is safe from action unless there are specific provisions to that effect in the documentation, although in some jurisdictions there are regulations or industry codes that require banks to pursue the assets of the borrower before they pursue guarantors.

- Most (but not all) types of facilities will incur default interest rates when they are in default. Facilities that are cross defaulted will also incur default interest from the time that the default applies (in some jurisdictions there are restrictions on the application of default interest to some types of facilities). Default interest rates are often quite punitive and can make a very significant difference to the level of debt.

- Banks are always entitled to recover the full amount of any costs incurred in seeking to recover their debt. These costs can be significant.

- Once you provide a personal guarantee for a debt facility of your business, someone else's business or another person, you are liable for the full amount of the debt that you have guaranteed, including default interest and any recovery costs, up to the limit of your guarantee. Your own facilities can be defaulted if one of the facilities that you have guaranteed goes into default. You cannot simply decide that you no longer wish to provide a guarantee, unless the original facility expires or that facility is changed in a material way without your consent. In the absence of the original facility expiring or a material variation being made to the facility, you will require the bank's consent if you wish to withdraw your guarantee.

Loan and security documentation will give the bank significant rights to seek to recover its debt. Borrowers and guarantors are generally in a fairly weak position legally once default has occurred. Understanding both your legal rights and obligations, and those of the bank, will assist you in understanding your negotiating position.

Banks do, however, have some vulnerabilities. These vulnerabilities potentially create a more even negotiating position, as discussed in the next section.

Understand the legal, ethical, and moral framework in which the bank operates

All banks are subject to laws and/or industry standards and/or codes of conduct that impose conditions upon the manner in which the bank conducts itself with its customers.

The regulatory framework within which a bank operates will be a combination of laws, regulations, decisions in legal cases (case law), and binding or voluntary industry standards, such as a code of conduct. This framework will vary from country to country and, in some places, from state to state. As such, it is not possible or practical to provide comprehensive information on the legal framework that might be applicable in your circumstances, but it is important to understand that there is a legal framework within which your bank must operate.

In general terms, the regulatory framework will impose standards of behaviour upon your bank. Those standards of behaviour will, in most cases:

- require full disclosure of the obligations taken on by borrowers and/or guarantors at the time the loan is taken out
- require loan and guarantee terms and conditions to be written in such a way that they are easy to understand

- seek to ensure that banks act reasonably and fairly in dealing with their customers
- seek to ensure that loan terms are not excessively punitive, unfair or unreasonable
- often require banks to follow a formal complaints resolution process to provide dissatisfied customers with a forum in which to have their complaints heard.

In some jurisdictions, banks may be required to go through a mediation process before they can take enforcement action. This is increasingly common for loans to vulnerable people and loans to farmers. Regulations may provide recourse to an independent arbitrator if there is a dispute.

You can generally find some guidance in relation to the obligations of your bank to its customers by searching the internet. Start with your bank's own webpage to see if they have a charter that sets out their standards of behaviour towards customers. In many jurisdictions there is a government regulator or ombudsman charged with the role of enforcing the legislation that regulates banking. This organisation will usually be able to either provide you with advice as to the regulatory framework in which your bank is operating or point you to where you can find this information. If your business is operating through a corporation there will also be corporations legislation that may contain options that provide temporary protection against, and/or delay enforcement action by, creditors and possibly your bank. Examples of this type of protection include Chapter 11 in the USA, administration in the UK, and voluntary administration in Australia and New Zealand.

There is also an ethical framework within which banks operate. This framework may be self-imposed or imposed by public opinion. Your bank may be sensitive to adverse publicity or reputational damage. Ethical or reputational considerations are most commonly linked to customers who are disadvantaged. This group may include people who are unable to speak the language, those who are sick or disabled, the elderly, or people who may be mentally impaired. It may also extend to circumstances where people have been placed at financial disadvantage through no fault of their own, such as through redundancy, family illness, natural disasters, pandemics or other circumstances beyond their control.

Banks are generally expected to demonstrate high ethical and moral standards in their dealings with customers. Increasingly, banks are experiencing adverse publicity and legal action initiated by regulators or customers (including class actions) based on claims of maladministration or unconscionable conduct. There are several common behaviours that give rise to allegations of improper conduct and attract criticism to banks. These include:

- over-charging or gouging with excessive fees and high default interest rates
- failure to make appropriate and adequate enquiries or to use appropriate skill in assessing the loan, leading to the conclusion that the borrower never had the capacity to repay the debt from the outset
- failure to ensure that vulnerable guarantors (spouses, parents, siblings) were not under duress when they guaranteed a loan and were fully aware of the risks they were taking on
- pursuing borrowers who have been impacted by events outside their control, such as natural disasters
- pursuing borrowers and guarantors who are vulnerable.

Understanding the ethical and moral framework within which a bank operates may assist in the construction of your workout plan. In some circumstances it may provide justification for forbearance or support. Alternatively, if you or a co-borrower are vulnerable, it may provide grounds for arguing for more favourable treatment.

Make sure you have a workable plan

One of the most common mistakes I have seen made by business managers who make proposals to their banks is the delivery of unworkable or unachievable plans. Your bank will closely scrutinise your plans in the context of the recent past performance of your business, their knowledge of your industry and your business, and their expectations of the business environment confronting your business going forward. As such, your plan will need to stand up to critical review and objective analysis.

It is common for forecasts to be built around delivering a profit outcome based on what management believes the bank wants to see. These are known as "bottom-up" forecasts, where you start with the desired profit and build up the profit and loss account to determine the level of sales required to achieve those profits. Such forecasts generally result in a forecast that includes substantial sales growth. It is unlikely that a bank will accept that a business with a history of slow sales growth, flat sales or falling sales is likely to be able to deliver a substantial increase in sales in the coming year. There will be occasions when such dramatic growth is justifiable, but on these occasions there is usually a major new contract or contracts on the table that support the forecast increase. Moreover, it is common for managers to forget about cash flow when they are preparing bottom-up forecasts. Substantial sales growth will generally require a significant lift in working capital funding. Managers presenting bottom-up forecasts often find their plans rejected by the bank because of the significant increased funding requirement.

Where banks have doubts about the plan submitted, they may bring in an independent adviser (at your cost) to review your plans and advise them on the integrity of the underlying assumptions, the capacity of management to deliver the forecast performance, and the risks involved from the bank's perspective.

Your plan should be capable of being successfully implemented without the need for abnormal assumptions to be accepted. Abnormal assumptions are not limited to sales growth; they can also extend to other measures of business performance such as increased gross profit margins and expense reductions. The message here is that your plan must be deliverable on reasonable analysis.

Your plan should also include measurable outcomes and key milestones identified along the way. Defining these outcomes and milestones will provide the bank with comfort that you have considered the important stages of the turnaround process and the milestone events that will define your progress towards the desired objectives. The outcomes and milestones will also provide a framework against which you can report (and the bank can monitor) the progress of the implementation of your turnaround plan.

Sell your plan to your bank

Once you have prepared your strategy plan you will need to convince your bank that your plan is worth pursuing. Always remember that when you are dealing with your bank you are dealing with a business. Whatever you deliver to the bank must withstand commercial scrutiny.

You will need to convince your bank that your strategy provides, as a minimum, no worse an outcome than they might expect to achieve by adopting an alternative strategy. As such, you will need to consider the alternatives available to the bank and how the outcomes from those alternatives compare to the outcomes that are expected from your plan. Your analysis of the outcomes from alternative strategies should be included in your submission to the bank and you should be able to support your plan as the best strategy – or at least explain why your strategy is better even if it doesn't deliver the best or fastest outcome. You will not always be able to be totally definitive in terms of the financial outcomes for the bank from alternative strategies. If possible, support your estimate of the financial outcomes from alternative strategies with independent verification such as valuation advice. Do not limit your analysis to financial outcomes but consider other issues that may be relevant to the bank, such as the potential loss of value if your assets fall under the control of an administrator, loss of employment opportunities in your community if your business fails, and reputational risks to the bank arising from these and other impacts of enforcement action by the bank. It is also worth considering and discussing in your submission the benefit of your cooperation in the implementation of the plan and the fact that you will obviously be more inclined to work hard at achieving the outcome sought if you are in control of the process and you have something to gain from successful implementation of your plan.

In circumstances where your plan is expected to deliver full repayment of the bank's debt, your bank will probably start from the position that it would prefer not to pursue enforcement action. The only better outcome for the bank will be an alternative strategy that will deliver the same outcome (full debt repayment) in a shorter timeframe or with greater certainty (remember that time is a risk factor). Where your plan is likely to deliver full repayment, your bank is only likely to pursue an alternative strategy where it has serious doubts about your plan and a high degree of comfort in an alternative strategy. The reasons for this are quite simple – enforcement action introduces additional costs that increase the risk of losses, exposes the bank to reputational risks, and deprives the bank of a customer (your business).

Where there is a high risk that the bank will incur a loss, the thought process in the bank is likely to be different. The focus will be upon minimising the losses that might be incurred by the bank. The bank will also start from a less supportive position as it may well assign responsibility for the probable loss to the management of the business. There will be circumstances where management will not be responsible for the likely losses; for example, events such as natural disasters or economic downturns. If your plan does not deliver the best outcome for the bank then you will need to convince the bank that it is in their interests to pursue your plan, notwithstanding the fact that the outcome for the bank will not be the most favourable one. There are a range of possible arguments you might use to support your plan to the bank as the preferred option in these circumstances. These might include the benefits of having existing management involved in the turnaround process, the potential loss of key staff, the benefits of customer retention, the negative impacts on asset values that might result from the appointment of an administrator, reputational risks to the bank that might flow from the appointment of an administrator to the business, the potential for existing management to deliver a faster outcome with greater certainty, the additional cost burden of an external administrator, and community benefits in terms of retained employment.

Do not rely on emotional pleas or allegations of unfair dealings unless you have solid grounds to do so. They will rarely be successful unless backed up by a sound case and the prospect of adverse media coverage or litigation. Such strategies are best kept as an absolute last resort, but should not be discounted if all else fails.

Communicate often and effectively

Perhaps the most important element of maintaining a sound relationship with your bank when your business is experiencing difficulties is the need for effective communication. This is particularly true when you are seeking, or have secured, the support of your bank for implementing a turnaround strategy. Effective communication builds trust and trust is a critical element of maintaining the support of your bank.

You should include in your plan a communication strategy identifying what information you intend to give to the bank during the course of your turnaround, and when you will give them that information. This information will include financial reports and progress towards milestone events, each of which should be reported against the outcomes and milestones set out in your plan.

Remember at all times that your bank is a business. They will be seeking to make commercial decisions having regard not only to your interests but also the interests of the bank. You may find that your bank may appear to be slow, perhaps bureaucratic, and at times pedantic or unhelpful. You may feel that they do not understand your circumstances and are not trying to understand your circumstances. Despite any such frustrations, you should always keep your communications on a professional level. If you have legitimate concerns about anything the bank is doing then you should be prepared to express those concerns – but do so in a manner that reflects, to the extent possible, a reasonable and objective view of the applicable circumstances.

Trying to manage a business that is in trouble is always difficult and stressful. Do not let any difficulties you experience with your bank become personal. Do not alienate your bank manager by becoming agitated, angry or aggressive or by making personal attacks on their integrity or character. Persevere with reasonable, calm and considered communication at all times.

Deliver what you promise

Once you secure the support of your bank for your turnaround plan it is really important that you deliver what you have promised. You should be fully committed to your plan and to the achievement of its objectives and timeframes. The importance of having a deliverable plan will become evident when you seek to implement that plan. If you have set unrealistic targets or unachievable timeframes, the flaws in your plan will soon be revealed.

The delivery of your plan, as promised, will enhance your credibility with the bank and their trust in your ability both to forecast the future performance of your business and manage the business to achieve targeted outcomes and timeframes. Conversely, material failure to deliver on your plan will undermine the bank's confidence in both your ability to forecast the future trading performance of the business and your skills as a manager.

However, it is highly likely that, despite your best efforts, there will be glitches in your plan and unforeseen external events will impact on your plan. Your bank will understand that no plan will go off perfectly. They will understand that unexpected events will occur and that some of these events may adversely impact upon your plan either in terms of its timing or its outcome. They will not understand if they find out belatedly that there has been a material event, about which they have not been informed, that has adversely impacted upon the timing or likely outcome of your plan. So, ensure that you are reporting to the bank in a timely manner, keeping them informed of any material events that may impact on the outcome of your plan, and being frank and honest in your communications with the bank.

Be prepared to monitor your own performance against your plan. Regularly update the forecasts to reflect the actual results achieved to date and any changes to milestone events and outcomes. Always remain focused on delivering the best possible outcome in the circumstances, having regard to the interests of all stakeholders.

12. Managing people

It is really important to maintain an awareness of the impacts of your circumstances and your actions upon others and upon yourself. It is about keeping your world in perspective and responding sensitively to others and to yourself.

Many business people live and breathe for their business. It is usually their only source of income and the focus of most of their waking hours. Usually, much of their personal wealth is also tied up in the business. Little wonder then that when a business gets into trouble the owners and managers of the business suffer. They become stressed and usually work even harder to try to remedy the problems.

Managing a business on the brink of collapse is the most difficult position a businessperson can find themselves in. It is a period when owners and managers are likely to be faced with some of the most difficult and unpalatable decisions of their lives. Sometimes the responsibilities, stresses and strains of managing a business though troubled times can cause the owners and managers of the business to lose their sense of perspective. It can become a vicious downward spiral with the business downturn creating personal problems that in turn cause personal turmoil at a critical time for the business – which just makes business problems worse, and so around it goes.

Managing employees

Employees are also likely to become very insecure when the business they work for is in trouble. Managers often seek to hide problems being experienced by the business from most of their staff, but no matter how much you try to hide your position from staff, they will soon become aware that something is wrong. Bad news moves like lightning through a workplace.

Your employees, more than any other group of creditors, have a vested interest in the survival of your business. They have a lot to lose if your business fails. Knowledge about the predicament of your business will undoubtedly make your employees uncertain about their future and fearful of losing their employment.

If you are faced with the decision about downsizing your workforce to reduce employee costs, you could consider asking your employees to collectively accept pay cuts, either on a temporary or permanent basis, to assist the business through its difficulties. If you do elect to go down this route, recognise that you will be unlikely to get 100% support and you will need to consider what to do with those employees who do not accept your proposals. Having all employees accept a pay cut as an alternative to making some of them redundant is a cost reduction strategy that has been used in the past; but it is only a solution where you wish to retain your existing workforce, which means that your turnaround strategy must include retaining most, if not all, of your existing productive capacity.

If you decide that a reduction in your workforce is necessary, making a quick decision about who will stay and who will go will assist in minimising disruption to staff and the business generally. This will also enable the position to be quickly and honestly communicated to employees – both those who are going and those who are staying – so that you can restore certainty, remove their fear of losing their employment, and avoid the consequential impacts of fear and uncertainty. Managing staff who are faced with redundancy is discussed next. If you have a unionised workforce, it will be necessary to engage with the union very early in the process. You will need to maintain active consultation to assist them in understanding the need for redundancies and the process that employees will experience.

Uncertainty about the future may cause some employees to leave and seek greater security of employment elsewhere. It is natural for people to respond in this manner, and it may well be that both parties are better off going their separate ways where the employee lacks confidence in the future of the business.

If you have critical employees who need to be retained, you should act early to reassure them about their employment and secure their commitment to the business. It is important that you bring along on the journey of turning your business around all employees who are staying. It is likely you will find that most of your employees will be willing to put in additional effort to help save the business and retain their jobs. A successful turnaround where employees feel that they have been part of the journey and the solution, can build trust and loyalty and team cohesion. You may well find that productivity improves and staff turnover declines after the turnaround process is completed.

Always treat your employees with respect and, where you asked them to go that extra mile to assist you during the turnaround process, recognise their contribution and their efforts.

Managing staff redundancies

It is usually the case that a successful turnaround involves a downsizing of the business and that generally means some employees will have to go. There is no easy or simple solution to delivering the message to an employee that their employment is to be terminated. People are always uncomfortable when they are confronted with uncertainty. Their jobs represent a very important part of their lives and, often, the primary source of their income. An employee faced with losing their job experiences an array of emotions. They may feel unloved, unwanted and unappreciated by their employer. Their expectation is that they will be socially, financially and personally impacted if they lose their job. They may be fearful about the difficulties of getting alternative employment and about meeting their financial commitments. In these circumstances, uncertainty works in tandem with fear. If there are individual employees in your organisation who you worry may not cope well with being made redundant, you might consider engaging a professional counselling service to provide them with advice on demand to assist them through this difficult period. You might also consider offering the employees who are being made redundant access to a transitional employment service that might offer advice on retraining, preparing resumes, applying for jobs, and participating in job interviews. Some of these agencies also offer office facilities and support services which are available to the terminated employees while they seek alternative employment.

It is important to treat employees who are being made redundant with dignity and respect. Deliver the message honestly and fairly, making it clear that the cause of the termination is the need to reduce costs to keep the business from failing. Make sure that they are fully compensated in accordance with the necessary redundancy provisions of their employment award or contract.

It is likely to be less painful for all concerned if the process of exiting the business is as quick and clean as possible. As some employees can become embittered when they are advised their employment will be terminated, it is important to remove access to critical business information immediately and to ensure that, after termination, access to business computer systems and premises is precluded. These are simple, sensible security measures that every business should take, whether or not the employee concerned is considered to be trustworthy and reliable. Withdrawal of access privileges should be handled with sensitivity.

If the process of terminating employees who are being made redundant is one that makes you feel particularly uncomfortable, you might consider engaging a professional human resources consultant to assist you through the process.

Your family

One of the most difficult decisions faced by managers of businesses that are experiencing serious problems is deciding how much of the burden to share with family. On the one hand, there is the desire not to worry the family about what might happen if the business fails. On the other hand, there is the need to share your story and seek their support or counsel to assist you through the process of coping with the stresses of trying to turn the business around. Sharing your circumstances with your partner (or a trusted friend if you don't have a partner) and telling them openly and honestly about what is being experienced in the business and what you are planning to do will help you to cope and make them feel a part of the journey, however difficult it might be. Your partner will want to share your feelings, your concerns and your aspirations. Take the opportunity to seek their support. Trust them with your feelings. Share the burden with them if they are willing to share the burden with you. It helps just to have someone to listen to your story and your plans. Often a confidant can bring a different perspective. Support from your partner can reinforce and reinvigorate your enthusiasm and motivation. If nothing else, your partner can be a sounding board for your thoughts, fears and frustrations.

Most business owners are dependent upon their business income to meet their personal financial commitments. A business that is having problems is often unable to provide sufficient cash to support both the obligations of the business and the financial obligations of the proprietors. Cash stress in the business usually means cash stress in the home.

It is not uncommon to see relationships damaged by conflicts driven by the financial and personal stresses caused by problems in the business. Many divorces have their origins in these circumstances. Be careful not to take your frustrations and fears out on your partner and your family. Don't mistake releasing your anger, frustrations, and fears with sharing. Make your interactions with your partner a positive, sharing experience. Don't expect them to have all the answers. Remember, they will be experiencing their own fears. Support one another.

Sharing your situation with your broader family is a subjective decision. It will depend upon your relationship with specific members of your broader family and the purpose for which you might consider involving them in the knowledge of the circumstances of your business. It may be that you have a relative who is experienced in business from whom you might seek advice, or other relatives who you believe might be willing to provide some financial support to your business. Again, be careful to manage family relationships carefully. Often, where a small business is concerned, there is little choice about involving family because they are already involved in the business, and therefore privy to the difficulties being faced.

At the end of the day your family is more valuable than your business. Protecting your family relationships through a period of financial difficulties requires that you respect your family, trust them, and manage your own responses to the stresses you will experience.

Managing yourself

Perhaps the most important learning is understanding the importance of managing your own responses to the problems impacting your business. You will multiply the prospects of success for your turnaround plan and be a better manager if you learn to manage yourself well in a crisis situation.

Owning and managing a failing business is an extremely stressful experience. Fear of failure, fear of public embarrassment, and fear of losing everything you have are natural but very stressful responses. Personal guilt and anger are also common emotional responses to finding yourself in these circumstances. It is quite normal to blame yourself for making mistakes that have led to the current situation and to be angry with yourself for allowing things to get this way. Confusion about what to do can add to the stress, as can frustration with impediments to resolving your situation. It is not unusual to experience conflicts with unhappy creditors, unhappy staff and sometimes with stressed partners, family and shareholders. Worry and stress are your constant companions.

It will come as no surprise to learn that managing a troubled business can sometimes lead to physical and emotional breakdown. Confronting all of these stress factors on a daily basis means you are likely to be stressed out, worrying constantly, confused, frustrated, and most unlikely to be sleeping well. Not a great formula for success!

You are the key to the success of your business. You are the person most committed to the success of your turnaround plan. You need to be at the top of your game to overcome the hurdles and challenges that face every manager of a business that is going through a significant downturn. You are the beacon your staff and family will look to for motivation and direction during their own periods of stress. Other stakeholders, such as your creditors and your bank, will also be looking at you, to judge your ability to deliver on your plan. The value of maintaining your own wellbeing cannot be emphasised enough. Do not believe that you need to be seen to be killing yourself with work to convince others of your commitment. It is not self-indulgence to manage your own wellbeing, it is good business.

Working relentlessly without any attempt to manage your physical and mental wellbeing is a recipe for failure. Do not live in the mistaken belief that the longer and harder you work the more likely you are to succeed in your efforts to turn your business around. You will quickly become ineffective, emotional, and indecisive as the constant stress, tiredness and physical exhaustion erode your capacity to work in an effective manner. This is not to say that trying to turn your business around will not require total commitment and hard work. It most certainly will. What I am saying is that management of your own physical and mental wellbeing is a critical part of any effective turnaround strategy.

In order to be effective as the manager of your business in troubled times you need three core competencies – a clear mind, a healthy body, and a positive, can-do attitude.

Keeping a clear mind

Maintaining a clear head is probably the most important activity you will undertake in the whole process of turning your business around – and one of the hardest. Without a clear head you will never fully realise your potential to develop and implement good strategies. One benefit you will find from taking your mind away from the problems of your business on a regular basis is that fresh ideas and solutions to problems will flow naturally into your mind. The human brain seems to have a knack for searching out solutions and answers while our conscious minds are elsewhere. Make sure that you have a pen and paper handy to write down any new ideas or solutions that come to you.

Maintaining a healthy body

Keeping your body in a healthy condition will both avoid the distraction of ill-health and assist you in keeping your mind focused. We all know that a healthy body comes from good nutrition, adequate rest, and exercise. In the case of someone trying to cope with business problems, managing stress, adequate sleep and avoiding excessive consumption of alcohol or stimulants (including nicotine) are important to maintaining good health. A sensible diet with regular meals will help, as will a regular, disciplined routine for physical activity.

Maintaining perspective

It is easy to let the stresses, guilt, conflicts, anger, and frustrations of a business in trouble get on top of you. If this occurs you can lose your perspective and things can get out of kilter. Adopting strategies to clear your mind and keep your body healthy will greatly help you to keep your circumstances in perspective. Sharing your feelings, thoughts and ideas with your partner will also help. If you still find yourself struggling to cope, take the initiative and get some professional help.

Everyone has their own way of relaxing, unwinding and relieving stress. Some will find family time important; for others exercise, yoga, meditation, reading or hobbies will be the answer. We all have different dietary and lifestyle habits, so diet and other lifestyle choices to optimise personal wellbeing will vary from person to person. You can work out a plan that suits your personal lifestyle, needs and preferences. There are plenty of good books, websites and professional advisers available to assist you in developing strategies to keep your body, mind and attitude in good condition. Take advantage of these resources and don't neglect yourself. Remember, you are critical to the success of your turnaround plan, so devoting resources to keeping yourself well mentally and physically is a very sound investment.

13. Exit strategies

Not every business can be turned around. Sometimes there are circumstances that are inherently fatal to a business. Sometimes a turnaround is not seen as a viable option for the current management team, current ownership, with the current equity base, or in the current economic circumstances. Sometimes turnaround plans don't work out as hoped, and sometimes the owners just get tired of battling with the difficulties of trying to turn their business around. Even though you may have decided not to embark upon, or continue with, a turnaround strategy, you will still need to develop and implement a plan to exit your business. An exit strategy will provide the opportunity to realise the maximum amount of value from the business, if any value remains to be realised. Any exit strategy must focus on three priorities:

1. **The financial outcomes of the strategy**. Any exit strategy will have financial implications for all stakeholders – employees, financiers, creditors, revenue authorities, and shareholders/partners. These stakeholders will be seeking to recover the maximum possible amount from the business. Financial outcomes will usually be the most significant priority in an exit strategy.

2. **The risks of the exit strategies being proposed**. All exit strategies will present challenges. The prospective financial outcomes will usually differ quite markedly depending upon the level of risk the proprietors are prepared to accept in realising the business or its assets.

3. **The timing of the exit process**. In any exit plan, time is a risk factor. The longer the exit strategy takes to complete, the more

it will cost and the greater the risk that something will change that will materially alter or impede the target outcomes.

There are a number of options available to exit your investment in the business. These options include selling the whole business, selling part of the business, selling the assets of the business, and liquidating the business. In some circumstances you may not have the luxury of time or adequate resources to implement an orderly exit strategy. The options available in these circumstances are considered in the next chapter.

Selling your business

The most obvious exit strategy is to sell all or part of your business as a going concern. Sale of part or all of the business may introduce new equity that may provide the opportunity for the business to be turned around and, ultimately, be successful.

There are several options available for selling part or all of your business. These include:

- a trade sale – where the whole business or an individual business unit is offered to other businesses in the same industry or in complimentary industries
- an open market sale – where the business is offered to any and all interested parties via a marketing campaign
- a management buyout ("MBO") – where the business is sold to existing management and staff
- a public listing – where shares in the business are offered to the public via a listing on a stock exchange.

Where a business is loss-making, the difficulties with a going concern sale are twofold – firstly, trading losses will need to be funded while the business is being sold and, secondly, businesses that are making trading losses usually have little or no value beyond the value of their assets. In the absence of goodwill, it is often more cost-effective to shut down the business and sell off its assets. The exception to this rule includes circumstances where there might be significant value in the customer base of the business, in which case sale of the business as a going concern may be preferable to a shut-down strategy.

Trade sale

A trade sale of the whole business or individual business units has advantages over other options available to sell part or all of your business. The most significant benefit of a trade sale is that it is usu-ally the quickest sale process because you are dealing with people who are either in the same industry or in compatible industries, where potential buyers will have a good understanding of the fun-damentals of the business and the issues around the industry. Trade buyers are often more enthusiastic than other buyers because they see the strategic opportunity represented by your business. As such, they will often be willing to pay a good price (even for a loss-making business) and to move more quickly to secure the opportunity than might be the case with other buyers. A quick sale is advantageous when the business being sold is loss-making.

Trade sales are usually undertaken using specialist divisions of major accounting firms, investment banks or stockbrokers to facilitate the sale. In some cases, it may be possible to approach potential buyers directly, if you know of one or two parties who may be keenly inter-ested in your business.

One risk in selling all or part of your business via a trade sale is that the sale process will inevitably involve the disclosure of information to your competitors that may be used to enhance their own busi-ness. There are some measures that may be taken to prevent or re-strict such activities by competitors, but it is difficult to secure highly sensitive information in a business sale process (this is equally true of an open market sale process). There is usually little more that can be done, other than to seek confidentiality agreements and contractual restrictions on the use of information disclosed during a sale process, to protect against these activities. Customer lists should not be provided to buyers until the sale is unconditional.

Open market sale

An open market sale obviously exposes your business to the widest range of potential buyers. This wide exposure offers the potential for a keen buyer to emerge from outside the industry or compatible industries. It also offers the potential for a buyer who may see the future of the industry or opportunities for the industry in a different way to current industry participants.

An open market sale will generally take longer than a trade sale and will often require a greater level of disclosure to, and due diligence by, prospective buyers. It is more common in an open market sale for part of the sale price to be tied to the future performance of the business.

Open market sales are generally undertaken by specialist business broking firms. In some industries there are specialist business brokers who concentrate on one specific business area such as pharmacies, aged care, medical practices, hotels or management letting rights.

Shutdown strategies

In some circumstances, the best way to realise value from your business is to shut it down and sell off the assets. A shutdown strategy is usually adopted where a business is unprofitable, and there is little or no goodwill in the business to result in a going-concern sale value exceeding the value of the assets of the business. Where a business is losing money, every day the business operates will cost money and reduce the recovery from the realisation of the business assets. Generally, this will occur where a loss-making business is facing insurmountable impediments to any material improvement in trading due to severe competition or a substantial, permanent loss of sales due to legislative or technological changes. In these circumstances, sale of the assets of the business is likely to be the best strategy to eliminate the erosion of value and equity caused by continuing trading losses.

Shutdown involves terminating all staff, decommissioning and selling all plant and equipment, selling off stock, collecting from debtors, and paying out creditors. Shutdown is often undertaken on a staged basis to avoid a sudden massive drain on cash flow as a result of having to pay out all the staff of the business in one go.

Even where a shutdown strategy is adopted, the sale of business assets as a whole may result in a better outcome than a piecemeal sale of assets. Potential purchasers may see value in the potential to upgrade the business to a competitive footing by upgrading equipment or technology.

There are two options in terms of a shutdown strategy. The first is a self-managed shutdown where the owners of the business undertake the shutdown process. The second is voluntary liquidation where an external administrator controls the shutdown process. Whether you elect to go with a self-managed shutdown or the appointment of a liquidator, you should seek independent legal and financial advice before starting the process so that you ensure the risks inherent in the process are understood and properly managed.

Be aware that shutting down a business is likely to trigger action by secured creditors to realise their securities so, if you do plan a shutdown strategy, it would be prudent to keep your secured lenders informed of your plans and seek their support for your strategy. You should also review the terms of your supply/credit contract with your suppliers, as some of these may entitle the creditor to pursue you for the debt and to take security over your personal assets.

SELF-MANAGED SHUTDOWN

This is the least expensive method, and is likely to result in the highest gross realisation due to the personal commitment and understanding of the management/ownership team. Obviously, this method involves significant work for the business owners and management team.

A self-managed shutdown should only be undertaken where you are highly confident that the total realisation from the assets of the business will exceed the liabilities of the business (or where you are prepared to make up any shortfall from your personal resources). There are many potential complications if there is a shortfall. If a shortfall is expected, it is likely that you will be advised to appoint a liquidator.

It is often the case that assets sold in the course of a shutdown process do not realise their expected value. There are many factors that can influence the prices received for assets sold in a shutdown. Among those that can have a negative impact are the costs of selling and relocating assets, prevailing market sentiment (if your business isn't making money, your competitors – who are also the most likely buyers of the assets of your business – may also be struggling), and the "bargain basement" mindset of buyers at trade sales and online auctions (these comments apply equally to a voluntary liquidation). Be conservative in your estimation of expected realisations and use expert advice where necessary to get some certainty around the outcome.

Remember to keep your secured and unsecured creditors aware of what you are doing, and why, and to seek their forbearance while you realise the assets of the business to pay them the monies they are owed.

VOLUNTARY WINDING UP/LIQUIDATION

The second option is a voluntary winding up of the business under the control of a liquidator. Under this scenario, an official liquidator is appointed by the company to conduct the winding up process. This option is a more costly option but provides directors with protection from the claims of unsecured creditors (except where insolvent trading has occurred prior to the appointment of the liquidator) if there is a shortfall between the amount realised from the sale of the assets of the business and the amounts owed to creditors. It also relieves the directors of the obligation of managing the realisation process.

14. Too late?

Insolvency

As the diagram in Chapter 2 illustrates, a business in decline spirals through stages which, if not stopped, will culminate in its ultimate failure. If a business is allowed to progress too far down the path towards failure, a turnaround strategy may not succeed. Implementing a successful turnaround strategy requires two critical inputs – time and money. You may find yourself in a position where there is insufficient time or money available to implement a turnaround strategy. Usually, this circumstance will be caused by a lack of cash to keep the business trading and/or to keep creditors at bay. Money can generally buy time but it will not guarantee a successful turnaround.

Some events will place a successful turnaround out of reach. Enforcement action by a secured creditor or successful legal action by unsecured creditors or taxation authorities may preclude any turnaround strategy. Legislative restrictions (and associated penalties) attaching to insolvent trading are another potentially serious impediment that may also give rise to some level of personal liability for the debts of the business.

A business is generally considered to be insolvent if it is unable to pay its debts as and when they fall due for payment. If your business is trading while insolvent, you are likely to be at risk of being held personally liable for debts incurred by the company while the business is insolvent. Some countries have legislation that provides a degree of protection to directors who continue to trade while the business is insolvent if they are pursuing a formal workout strategy.

You should seek advice from a suitably qualified lawyer or accountant to ensure you fully understand the legal position if you continue to trade your business when there is uncertainty around its ability to meet its obligations.

Voluntary options for an insolvent business

Voluntary administration/statutory protection/Chapter 11 bankruptcy

Company, bankruptcy or insolvency laws in your jurisdiction are likely to provide the opportunity, via some form of external administration, for short-term relief from action by creditors and/or landlords in certain circumstances. The specific features of these laws vary from country to country but, generally speaking, most developed countries have laws that offer businesses the opportunity to enter into some form of restructuring arrangements, or interim administration, to provide a window of opportunity to save the business. These laws usually offer a "standstill" or freezing of the financial position of a business while an external administrator and the creditors of the business have the opportunity to consider whether or not there are acceptable strategies available to save the business. This means that during a hiatus period, determined by the relevant laws, unsecured creditors may be precluded from seeking to have the business wound up and, in some instances, suppliers, lenders and landlords are precluded from seeking to recover possession of their property or security for a short standstill period. Secured creditors (banks or other financiers that hold direct security charges over the assets of the business) may not be bound by these standstill arrangements in all jurisdictions.

Under these laws, an administrator will assess the position of the business and make recommendations to creditors as to the options available to keep the business trading. It is possible, with the support of creditors, for a business to go through an extended turnaround process that may last for a number of years. It is usual for these turnaround plans to be controlled by an external administrator, or subject to external monitoring, with regular overview and reporting requirements. Control of the business will usually be returned to the directors upon successful completion of the turnaround. Alternatively, if the creditors cannot agree on the proposed turnaround plan, if no suitable turnaround plan is submitted, or if the turnaround plan fails, the business will be wound up and a liquidator will be appointed by creditors.

An alternative to voluntary administration, in circumstances where there is no potential merit in continuing to trade a business, is to voluntarily wind up the business via the appointment of a liquidator.

Due to jurisdictional variations, it is not possible to provide a detailed examination of the exact nature and application of these laws. You should seek independent legal and/or financial advice from a suitably qualified and experienced practitioner with respect to the process to ensure that the statutory requirements are satisfied, and that the risks inherent in the process are fully understood.

Phoenix arrangements

The phoenix was a mythical bird that rose from the ashes. In a similar way, some business owners have sought to avoid the liabilities of their business by liquidating the entity through which their business operates, only to re-emerge operating the same business in a different entity soon after. The outcome of these arrangements is that the creditors of the former business lose out, and the business owner emerges with essentially the same business without the burden of the creditors. These "phoenix" arrangements are illegal in most jurisdictions. There are similar arrangements, which may not be illegal in some jurisdictions, referred to as "pre-packs". In these arrangements, the purchase of the business by its former owners is pre-arranged with the liquidator. If you are advised to consider such arrangements, please ensure that you take good legal advice to ensure that you do not end up breaking the law.

Forced liquidation

Laws in every jurisdiction will provide for creditors, taxation authorities or government bodies to seek the wind up of a business where debts remain unpaid. The process usually requires a demand for payment to be issued and, if the demand is unsatisfied, applying to the relevant court or authority for an order requiring the wind up of the business.

If this occurs, you will lose control of your business immediately upon the appointment of the liquidator, who will assume the powers of the directors of the business. Existing directors will lose all authority. The liquidator will be charged with responsibility for realising the assets of the business and distributing the net proceeds to creditors. The liquidator will usually have primary responsibility and accountability to the creditors of the business.

If you find yourself in the position where a liquidator has been appointed to your business you will have no control and so will not be able to implement a turnaround plan. Your only options will be to challenge the appointment of the liquidator in court or to seek to extract the business from liquidation.

If you consider the appointment of the liquidator by the court should not have occurred, you should seek legal advice to determine if this route is worth pursuing. It is likely to be difficult, expensive and risky to pursue overturning a court decision.

Extracting the business from liquidation will require purchasing the business or key assets from the liquidator to enable you to restart the business in another entity or repay all the liabilities of the business.

You should seek expert advice on your options and to assist you to develop your strategy if you find a liquidator has been appointed to your business. It is important that you have an up-to-date understanding of the actions proposed by the liquidator and the timing of those actions. You should also seek to open and maintain communications with the liquidator.

15. Make sure it never happens again

Once your turnaround plan has been successfully implemented, you will need a strategy to ensure that you never allow your business to fall into decline again. This will involve a series of actions and strategies that should become a part of your business management routine going forward. It is easy to relax and take your eye off the ball after all the stress and strain of working through a turnaround and to put off implementing ongoing strategies to avoid any recurrence.

Manage risk

Continue to take time out of the day-to-day activities of your business to manage and review the threats to your business and how well you are managing, or are prepared to manage, those risks. You should continue to use the threat matrix (Chapter 7) to monitor and evaluate risks on a regular basis.

Be proactive in managing risks as they emerge so that they never get to become serious problems.

Keep proper accounting records

Timely preparation of management accounting reports is an essential element of good business management. You can use an off-the-shelf program such as QuickBooks or MYOB to maintain your accounting records or have your accountant prepare the records and reports.

Producing a profit and loss account and balance sheet on a monthly or quarterly basis will provide you with visibility of the trading performance of your business, a source of trend analysis, and a basis for future planning.

Use your financial reports to understand your business better

Take the time to understand what these reports are telling you about your business – in particular, about sales, profit margins, overheads, and the other cash drivers of your business (stock, debtors, creditors, and capital expenditure). Monitor and respond to trends in these drivers, especially adverse trends, that continue over two or three accounting periods.

Plan

You should make planning a regular part of your business processes. Planning will involve reviewing what you have done, the environment that your business is operating in, and changes you expect to occur in the next planning period. This process will help you to see emerging trends, evaluate the operations of your business, and focus your attention on the operating environment going forward and the future outlook both at a business and broader economic level.

At a high level, you should map where you want to take your business and how you plan to get there. This is strategic planning. You should have a strategic plan that is reviewed annually and updated for changes to your business, the market, and the economic environment.

An integral part of your annual planning should also be the preparation of financial forecasts. Try to develop three-way forecasts incorporating profit and loss, balance sheet, and cash flow forecasts. Three-way forecasts allow you to understand and forecast not only key profit and loss measures but changes in all of the cash drivers (stock, debtors, creditors, sales, gross profit margin, overheads, and capital expenditure). This will also enable you to understand the funding requirements of your business so that you can begin discussions with your bank before you start to run out of cash.

In order to prepare reliable three-way forecasts you will need accurate historical financial reports to rely upon. This is one reason why proper financial records are important to effective management, sustainable profitability and a strong balance sheet.

Ensure that you make use of your plan by regularly (no less often than quarterly) reviewing progress and updating your plan and forecasts as circumstances change.

Build resilience

Part of your strategy should be to build the capacity of your business to weather economic downturns and other unforeseen events. Resilience is strengthened by:

- keeping debt within moderate limits. While debt can facilitate growth it also represents a risk when things turn bad. The correct balance of debt and equity will allow you to sleep easily when the inevitable tough times re-emerge. Most large, publicly listed businesses have debt of less than 30% of total assets, meaning that 70% or more of the value of the business is funded by equity. This will provide you with some guidance as to where you should be headed with debt
- having a management succession plan (or an exit strategy if you intend to exit the business when you have had enough)

- building a solid team (including external advisers) and not allowing material dependency on key staff to develop (including yourself). Always have a backup for every role, even if it is only achieved by cross-training people
- developing a culture of identifying and managing threats on a constant basis so you can respond quickly to any emerging threats
- staying lean and avoiding excesses. There is always a tendency to relax and allow expenses to grow when times are good. Make sure you keep your costs under control and manage them carefully to avoid allowing your business to get lazy and fat. You will only be opening the door to competitors if you allow this to happen. Don't go overboard with personal expenditure and personal debt unless you are very comfortable with either your financial position or the capacity of the business to support its own needs, and yours. Many a businessperson has encountered problems because they have over-geared personally and placed a heavy burden on their business.

Most importantly, continue to manage your own wellbeing. Without your physical and mental health, it will all have been for nothing. Try to make time for your family and friends. Always be mindful of the support you have received from others. Avoid divorce and the other deadly D's (Chapter 1) if you can. Try to practise careful listening, respect for others, and always doing the right thing.

About the author

Steve Lloyd had his first experience with business failure in 1976, when the business he joined upon leaving university went broke. That business had been established more than 30 years. Fourteen years later, during a serious economic downturn, he began his long involvement with distressed businesses, when he found himself managing a team of bankers dealing with a large group of businesses that were experiencing financial difficulties. The downturn was so severe that the bank itself suffered serious losses and was ultimately split up and sold off. For the following seventeen years Steve was a consultant, advising and managing businesses through varying stages of the distress cycle, before joining a major Australian bank as a specialist workout banker to assist with the fallout from the Global Financial Crisis. In that role he has routinely managed a rotating portfolio of 20–30 small to medium distressed businesses in a wide variety of industries, as well as mentoring and training younger bankers.

Survive in Business (surviveinbusiness.com) has been spawned from these experiences, which led Steve to believe that many business failures can be avoided by educating and supporting business managers in their understanding of the causes of business failure and the practices and processes to remedy them. It is his goal to equip business managers with the skills and knowledge to effectively manage their businesses through periods of distress, and to build their understanding of how to make their businesses stronger and more resilient.

Acknowledgements

This book would not have been possible without the unfailing support of my wife, Margaret, to whom I am grateful for her love, patience, wisdom and an alternative perspective. I also wish to thank my managing editor, Belinda Pollard, for enlightening me on the mysteries of publishing and for the advice and support she, together with editor Alix Kwan, have provided.

www.ingramcontent.com/pod-product-compliance
Lightning Source LLC
Chambersburg PA
CBHW071157210326
41597CB00016B/1581